I0102558

Cow Dung

FOR
FOOD SECURITY
AND
SURVIVAL OF HUMAN
RACE

By
Dr. Sahadeva dasa

B.com., FCA., AICWA., PhD
Chartered Accountant

Soul Science University Press

Readers interested in the subject matter of this
book are invited to correspond with the publisher at:
SoulScienceUniversity@gmail.com   +91 98490 95990
or visit DrDasa.com

First Edition: September 2014

Soul Science University Press expresses its gratitude to the
Bhaktivedanta Book Trust International (BBT), for the use of quotes by
His Divine Grace A.C.Bhaktivedanta Swami Prabhupada.

ISBN 97893-82947-12-7

Published by:
Dr. Sahadeva dasa for Soul Science University Press

Printed by:
Rainbow Print Pack, Hyderabad

To order a copy write to purnabramhadasa@gmail.com
or buy online: Amazon.com, rlbdeshop.com

They are now killing animal, but animal lives on this grass and grains. When there will be no grass, no grains, where they will get animal? They'll kill their own children and eat. That time is coming. Nature's law is that you grow your own food. But they are not interested in growing food. They are interested in manufacturing bolts and nuts.
-Srila Prabhupada (Morning Walk, June 22, 1974, Germany)

By The Same Author

Oil-Final Countdown To A Global Crisis And Its Solutions

End of Modern Civilization And Alternative Future

To Kill Cow Means To End Human Civilization

Cow And Humanity - Made For Each Other

Cows Are Cool - Love 'Em!

Let's Be Friends - A Curious, Calm Cow

Wondrous Glories of Vraja

We Feel Just Like You Do

Tsunami Of Diseases Headed Our Way - Know Your Food Before Time Runs Out

Cow Killing And Beef Export - The Master Plan To Turn India Into A Desert

Capitalism Communism And Cowism - A New Economics For The 21st ` Century

Noble Cow - Munching Grass, Looking Curious And Just Hanging Around

World - Through The Eyes Of Scriptures

To Save Time Is To Lengthen Life

Life Is Nothing But Time - Time Is Life, Life Is Time

Lost Time Is Never Found Again

Spare Us Some Carcasses - An Appeal From The Vultures

An Inch of Time Can Not Be Bought With A Mile of Gold

Career Women - The Violence of Modern Jobs And The Lost Art of Home Making

Cow Dung – A Down To Earth Solution To Global Warming And Climate Change

Corporatocracy - You Are A Corporate Citizen, A Slave of Invisible And Ruthless Masters

Working Moms And Rise of A Lost Generation

Glories of Thy Wondrous Name

India A World Leader in Cow Killing And Beef Export - An Italian Did It In 10 Years

As Long As There Are Slaughterhouses, There Will Be Wars

Peak Soil – Industrial Civilization, On The Verge of Eating Itself

If Violence Must Stop, Slaughterhouses Must Close Down

(More information on availability on DrDasa.com)

Contents

Preface

We have taken our food for granted and many of us have no idea where it comes from. Jennifer Hill from Bristol recalls, "Several years ago I took my daughter and her friend to our allotments. As we left I dug up a couple of bunches of my prized organic carrots and offered one of them to my daughter's friend. With a look of absolute disgust the young girl said, 'My mommy doesn't get food from the dirt! She goes to Tescos!' Still, at least she knew what a carrot was."

Ask any child where their food comes from, and the chances are he or she will say the supermarket.

And most adults don't know a lot more about how food ends up on their plate either.

In our concrete, day-to-day experience it seldom comes to our awareness that our food is a gift, a blessing from beyond. This is so because all food originates from reproducing plant life – life that God created. It takes soil, water, air and sunlight for plants to grow, and the animals that become our food are dependent on this same plant life, air, water, and sunlight. Out of these ingredients, a crucial ingredient, soil is degrading at an accelerating pace and little is being done to rectify the situation. We are treating this critical resource as dirt.

We are trying to fool nature, forgetting that nature can not be fooled. Willian Lines warns, " For, although people can be fooled, tricked, and beguiled, nature can not. Material reality resists importuning, finessing, or re-negotiation. Nature's machinery is invariant, not subject to legislation or cultural conditioning. It can not be compromised."

Civilization survives on an ample supply of food and all previous civilizations developed near a food source. When farm productivity declined, usually as a result of soil mismanagement, civilizations also declined - and occasionally vanished entirely.

Today, all over the world, more than seven and a half million acres of soil has been degraded. That's larger than the U.S. and Canada combined. What remains is ailing as a result of compaction, erosion and salination making it near impossible to plant and adding to greenhouse gases and air pollution. Soil degradation is putting the future of the global population is at risk according to a National Geographic article by Charles Mann. Civil unrest in Latin America, Asia and Africa have been attributed to a lack of food and affordable food as a result of poor soil.

Any layman can understand the vital importance of topsoil as a rare and non-renewable resource which sustains all life on the planet. It is considered non-renewable because it takes centuries, if not millenniums to form one centimeter of top soil whereas it can be squandered in a matter of few decades.

We need to heed the warning and solutions presented in this book if we are at all serious about turning these trends around and building a safer, sustainable future.

Sahadeva dasa

Dr. Sahadeva dasa
1st September 2014
Secunderabad, India

1

Civilization

Survives On An Ample Supply of Food

Food is our common ground, a universal experience. If you're happy, you eat. If you're sad, you eat. You lose a job, you eat. You get a job, you eat. Therefore the bread is rightly called 'the staff of life'.

Civilization as it is known today could not have evolved, nor can it survive, without an adequate food supply.

It's amazing how pervasive food is. Every second commercial is for food. Every second TV episode takes place around a meal. In the city, you can't go ten feet without seeing or smelling a restaurant. There are 20 feet high hamburgers up on billboards.

But there is trouble with our food today. Traditional societies had good food but we just have good table manners. Our progress is unfortunately destroying this important aspect of our existence. There is even a saying that if you're going to America, bring your own food.

We have taken food for granted. Its a mistake for which we are paying dearly. Food doesn't grow on supermarket shelves.

A disease tsunami is sweeping the world. Humanity is dying out. This is the result of our deep ignorance about our food.

When you have your health you have everything. Most people who are sick and dying would trade all their possessions to feel better and live longer. When they toast each other, no matter what the language, it's usually some variant of, "to your good health." There's nothing more important.

If you don't have good health, the other things like food, housing, transportation, education and recreation don't mean much.

Its time to realize that so long as you have food in your mouth, you have solved all questions for the time being.

Civilizations Developed Near A Food Source

All the great cultures we hear about today were built along the great rivers systems like Nile, Ganges or Yangtze.

The rivers watered their crops and maintained their animals. Every year, the rivers flooded the Basin, refreshing the soil with rich silt and providing water for irrigation for miles on each side.

Without this annual renewal (thought by the ancient Egyptians to be the personal work and responsibility of the Pharaoh himself) the soil of the Basin would soon be exhausted and incapable of supporting the crops.

These cultures dating back to the beginning of time have relied on these stretches of water for everyday living. As a result, some of the most important events in history occurred along their shores. Even today, these rivers continue to support life, including your own. As goods are transported, crops are irrigated, and power is

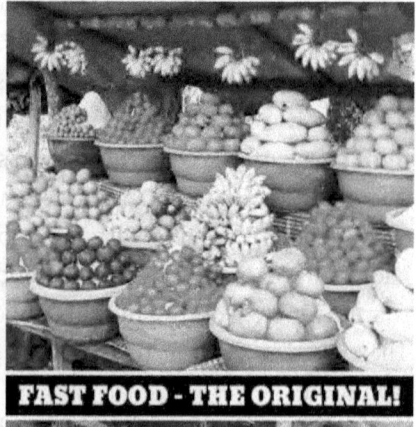

FAST FOOD - THE ORIGINAL!

created, nearly every person on the planet is affected by these rivers.

As such, it is no surprise that most major cities lie on the banks of a significant river, including the cities like Paris, London, Boston, Cairo, and Vienna.

The river Jordan is mentioned 175 times in the Old Testament. It played an important role in the everyday life of ancient Biblical society. But first and foremost, it was the supply of food.

Not surprising, when you consider the impact of rivers on agriculture and commerce, rivers often determined the political boundaries as well. The natural geography of the land was often used to designate political borders. Consider the Mississippi river with bisects the United States, drawing many state lines with its riverbanks. This is also true in Europe; the Danube was originally a border for the Roman Empire, and now designates the separation between modern Bulgaria and Romania.

Civilizations Declined With The Decline In Food Availability

When farm productivity declined, usually as a result of soil mismanagement, civilizations also declined - and occasionally vanished entirely.

Of the three requisites for a thriving civilization: fertile soil, a dependable water supply and relatively level land with reasonable rainfall which would not cause erosion, it is likely that the third factor was most important, and evidence is mounting that soil degradation has toppled civilizations as surely as military conquest. In countries bordering the Mediterranean, deforestation of slopes and the erosion that followed has created man-made deserts of once productive land. Ancient Romans ate well on produce from North African regions that are desert today.

annad bhavanti bhutani
parjanyad anna-sambhavah
yajnad bhavati parjanyo
yajnah karma-samudbhavah
All living bodies subsist on food grains, which are produced from rains.
Rains are produced by performance of yajna [sacrifice], and yajna is born
of prescribed duties.
  ~ Bhagavad-gita 3.14

A recent study of the collapse in Guatemala around 900 AD of the 1700 year-old Mayan civilization suggests that it fell apart for similar reasons. Researchers have found evidence that population growth among the Mayans was followed by cutting trees on mountainsides to expand areas for farming. The soil erosion that resulted from growing crops on steeper and steeper slopes lowered soil productivity - both in the hills and in the valleys - to a point where the populations could no longer survive in that area. Today only empty ruins remain.

Reference

FAO Corporate Document Repository, Natural Resources Management and Environment Department

Cristi Cave. "How a River Flows". Stream Biology and Ecology.

O'Neill, Ian. Titan's 'Nile River' Discovered 12 December 2012

Earth is here so kind, that just tickle her with a hoe and she laughs with a harvest.
~ Douglas Jerrold

2

Food

Comes From The Topsoil

Not From Our Factories

Top soil is the most important national resource because this is where our food comes from. Importance of top soil preservation can be understood by the example of an apple.

Let's think of Earth as an apple. Now Cut the apple into quarters. Set the three 'water' sections aside' and the remaining quarter represents the total land surface.

Slice the land (the remaining 1/4) in half, lengthwise. This 1/8 represents the half of the Earth's surface that is inhospitable to

people and to crops: the polar regions, deserts, swamps, and high or rocky mountains.

Set that 1/8 aside and take the other 1/8 piece. This 1/8 represents the other half of the Earth's surface. These are the areas on which people can live, but cannot necessarily grow food.

Slice this 1/8 crosswise into four equal pieces. Set aside 3 pieces, i.e., 3/32 parts. These 3/32 represent land on which people can live, but cannot grow food. Some of it was never arable because it's too rocky, wet, cold, steep or has soil too poor to produce food. Some of it used to be arable but isn't any longer because it's been developed—turned into cities, suburbs, highways, etc., so it can

Anna means food grains. Either animal or man, they must eat sufficiently. Either you eat grass or you eat rice or wheat or oats, in Sanskrit language these are called anna. Anna means foodgrains. So annad bhavanti bhutani [Bg. 3.14]. Every living entity lives. Nowadays there are scarcity of foodgrains. Even the human being cannot eat sufficiently, what to speak of animals. But formerly the kings, they used to maintain elephants. They were supplied very nice capatis. Do you know that? Still there are kings, they have elephants. Therefore elephant can be maintained by very rich man. If suppose, if somebody comes, he says, "Take this elephant, I give you free," will you take? Will you accept? You know that elephant will devour all your means or family income. Therefore in India sometimes, when, a hundred years ago, some students would come from England, especially London, and bring an European, English wife... In old days they were doing that. So people would say that "This man is maintaining one white elephant." Because a European wife means great expenditure (Laughter).

Annad bhavanti bhutani. Bhutani means embodied, those who have taken, accepted material bodies. They live by eating anna, either animal or human being. You require anna. Produce foodgrains. Foodgrains or grass or anything, whatever the animals and man eat, you must produce. And that production is there on the ground, not you factory. Not in the Birmingham factories. There are many factories in Birmingham? You cannot produce foodgrains there.

~ Srila Prabhupada (Lecture, Srimad Bhagavatam 1.10.4, London, November 25, 1973)

no longer be farmed. Governments have earmarked other areas, such as parks, nature preserves and other public lands to remain undeveloped forever.

So, only 1/32 of the Earth's surface has the potential to grow the food needed to feed all of the people on Earth.

Now carefully peel the 1/32 slice of Earth.

This tiny bit of peel represents the topsoil, the dark, nutrient-rich soil that holds moisture and feeds us by feeding our crops.

Reference

National Farmers Union, "Planet Stewardship", Section 3

Cooper, Elmer L. Agriscience, Fundamentals & Applications. 2nd ed. Albany, N.Y.: Delmar, 1995.

Soil

A Non-renewable Resource

It Is Practically Irreplaceable

Any layman can understand the vital importance of topsoil as a rare and non-renewable resource which sustains all life on the planet. It is considered non-renewable because it takes centuries, if not millenniums to form one centimeter of top soil whereas it can be squandered in a matter of few decades.

On our scale of time, soil formation is extremely slow. Where the climate is moist and warm, it takes thousands of years to form just a few centimetres of soil. In cold or dry climates, it takes even longer, or soil may not form at all. While soil is technically a renewable resource, its slow rate of formation makes it practically irreplaceable.

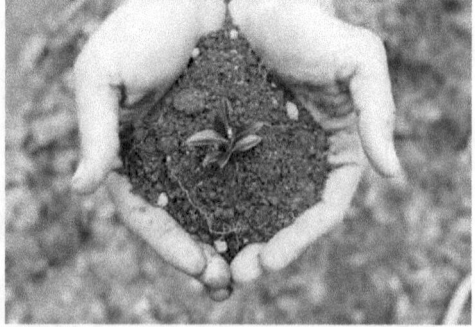

Soil covers most of the land surface of the earth in a thin layer, ranging from a few centimeters to several metres deep. It is composed of rock and mineral particles of many sizes mixed with water, air, and living things, both plant and animal, and their remains.

Soil is a dynamic mixture, forever changing as water comes and goes and plants and animals live and die. Wind, water, ice, and gravity move soil particles about, sometimes slowly, sometimes rapidly. But even though a soil changes, the layers of soil stay much the same during one human lifetime unless they are moved or scraped, or ploughed by man.

Reference:

Keeping the Land Alive: Soil Erosion--its Causes and Cures, Issue 50, By Hubert W. Kelley

Steven C. Hodges. Soil fertility Basics, Chapter 1, basic concepts. Soil Science Extention, North Carolina University.

On rising from the bed, a prayer is offered to Mother Earth:
samudra-vasane devi parvata-stana-mandite
visnu-patni namas tubhyam pada-sparsam ksamasva me
O Mother Earth, I offer my humble obeisances unto you, who are the
wife of Lord Visnu and the residence of the oceans, and who are decorated
with mountains. Please forgive me for stepping upon you.

Soil

Lifeline of A Nation

Why should the leaders of countries today commit their government and their people to a national programme of soil conservation?

The answer is that with the loss of soil goes man's ability to grow food crops and graze animals, to produce fibre and forests. It is not enough to describe the soil as a country's greatest source of wealth; it is more than that; it is a country's life. And in one country after another today, the soil is washing or blowing away and being destroyed by dangerous chemicals.

On the earth we can see so many living entities are coming out, beginning from the grass, then so many insects, reptiles, big trees, then animals, birds, beasts, then human beings. They are all coming from the earth, and they are living at the expense of earth. The earth is supplying food to everyone. As the mother gives life or maintains the child by the milk of her breast, similarly, the earth mother is maintaining all different types of living entities. There are 8,400,000 different forms of life, and the earth, mother earth is supplying food. There are thousands of elephants in the African jungle, they are also being supplied with food. And within your room in a hole there are thousands of ants, they are also being supplied food by the mercy of the Supreme Personality of Godhead. So the philosophy is that we should not be disturbed by the so-called theory of over-population. If God can feed elephants, why he cannot feed you? You do not eat like the elephant. So this theory, that there is a shortage of food or overpopulation, we do not accept it. God is so powerful that He can feed everyone without any difficulty. Simply we are mismanaging. Otherwise there is no difficulty.

~ Srila Prabhupada (Ratha-yatra -- New York, July 18, 1976)

Soil Degradation

An International Emergency

And The World's Most Critical Issue

Modern farming practices are utterly destructive as far as top soil is concerned. Scorched with chemicals, topsoil is getting destroyed and land is turning into a desert. Soil, deprived of farmyard manure, is in revolt.

Industrial civilization in last 200 years has been using up resources which took nature millions of years to create. This rate of resource usage is unsustainable. Unless we change our course, we are in for some serious trouble. There are concerns expressed about resources like fossil fuels, marine life, forest covers and mineral wealth but top soil escapes the attention of one and all. Policy makers and scientists don't know much and don't care either about this critical resource.

All over the world, more than seven and a half million acres of soil has been degraded. That's larger than the U.S. and Canada combined. What remains is ailing as a result of compaction, erosion and salination making it near impossible to plant and adding to greenhouse gases and air pollution. Soil degradation is putting the

"What you take from the earth, you must give back. That's nature's way."
~ Chris d'Lacey

future of the global population is at risk according to a National Geographic article by Charles Mann. Civil unrest in Latin America, Asia and Africa have been attributed to a lack of food and affordable food as a result of poor soil.

Experts estimate that by 2030 the Earth's population will reach 8.3 billion. Farmers will need to increase food production but not much soil remains. Of course, we already grow enough food but most of it is going to animal farming, rather than feeding humans.

Soil is the Earth's fragile skin that anchors all life. Soil is the most important national asset and its conservation deserves the highest national priority. Any civilization is founded on topsoil and soil erosion destroys it. Policy makers are blissfully unaware of this fact and national policies are being made in boardrooms as parliaments take a backseat.

Mother Earth is abused in Kali-yuga in many ways. When Kali-yuga began, Maharaja Pariksit found a sudra beating the earth personified, who appeared in the form of a cow. Nowadays the earth is drilled recklessly for oil, deforested, blown up, polluted by chemicals, stripped of fertile topsoil, and filled up with cheaters and liars who create an intolerable burden.

The earth is not a dead mass to be exploited by the human species; rather, she is a living entity meant to be protected. When the earth is protected, she gives ample space and a peaceful and prosperous residence for all living entities.

~ Srila Prabhupada (Narada Bhakti Sutra - 71)

Decline in National Food Self-sufficiency

Most of the countries in the world are slipping from self-sufficiency into import dependency.

13 nations specified in National Security Study Memorandum 200 (NSSM-200), prepared under Henry Kissinger in 1974, were analyzed with regards to food self-sufficiency.

By 1990, there were significant drops in food self-sufficiency over the prior 27-year period. In 1963, Mexico was 100% self-sufficient in grains output; it was a grains-exporting nation. As of 1990, Mexico was only 79% self-sufficient, i.e., a grains importing nation. The situation is even worse today.

Elsewhere in the Western Hemisphere, Brazil was about 90% self-sufficient in cereals in 1963, but dropped to 76% self-sufficient in 1990. Colombia remained about the same, staying at only 86-87% self-sufficient. Other nations in Ibero-America saw drastic declines in basic grains self-sufficiency. For example, Haiti, in 1970, was close to 95% self-sufficient; but, as of 1990, self-sufficiency had dropped down to 45%.

In Africa, Egypt was 84% self-sufficient in cereals production in 1963, and only 62% self-sufficient in 1990. Ethiopia was over 100% self-sufficient in grains supply in 1963, and dropped down to 81% self-sufficient in 1990. Nigeria remained at 99% self-sufficiency in grains the entire period but grains declined markedly as a component of the daily diet. Other locations in Africa saw drastic declines in grain self-sufficiency. For example, Algeria was 76% self-sufficient in grains in 1970; in 1990, Algeria was only 44% self-sufficient.

On the Asian subcontinent, India, which has moved from 96% in 1963 to 93% sufficiency at present, and Pakistan, has stayed at the 93-95% level. Bangladesh has gone from 106% grains self-sufficiency in 1963, down to 87%, and is subject to wide swings from year to year in grains supplies.

In Southeast Asia, wide annual swings in staple grains are also now common. In 1963, Indonesia was 89% self-sufficient in cereals; in 1990, it was 100% self-sufficient. But in several years since then, it has fallen back to rely on imports. Similarly, the Philippines stayed at 80-83% self-sufficiency levels for 1963 and 1990, but in recent years has seen growing dependency because of shortfalls in rice. Thailand, from which the cartel trading companies export many kinds of commodities (corn, livestock feed, meat, processed foods, etc.), was 159% self-sufficient in cereals in 1963, and 131% in 1990.

The United States, Canada, Australia, France, South Africa, and Argentina, these six nations together are the origin for a large

TABLE 1
National food self-sufficiency declines, 1963-90
100% = food self-sufficiency; under 100% = deficit; more than 100% = surplus

Nation	Cereals 1963	Cereals 1990	Pulses 1963	Pulses 1990	Oils 1963	Oils 1990	Milk 1963	Milk 1990
WESTERN HEMISPHERE								
Mexico	100%	79%	104%	85%	110%	57%	87%	68%
Brazil	89%	76%	100%	96%	105%	118%	96%	96%
Colombia	86%	87%	100%	76%	79%	94%	91%	79%
AFRICA								
Egypt	84%	62%	112%	88%	103%	90%	92%	93%
Ethiopia	104%	81%	100%	100%	142%	102%	99%	95%
Nigeria	99%	99%	100%	99%	207%	102%	82%	69%
INDIAN SUBCONTINENT								
India	96%	105%	100%	94%	100%	103%	98%	100%
Pakistan	95%	93%	100%	95%	108%	86%	99%	99%
Bangladesh	106%	87%	100%	88%	71%	83%	95%	83%
SOUTHEAST ASIA								
Indonesia	89%	100%	100%	88%	111%	96%	59%	75%
Philippines	83%	80%	97%	47%	266%	110%	6%	3%
Thailand	159%	131%	128%	171%	109%	101%	3%	75%
EURASIA								
Turkey	113%	99%	105%	140%	100%	99%	100%	98%
China	96%	99%	95%	111%	100%	100%	89%	100%
U.S.S.R.	87%	89%	100%	100%	94%	90%	100%	100%

Source: FAO Agrostats

percentage of the total tonnages of food products that the commodities cartels control and use to dominate world trade and food supplies.

Reference

Executive Intelligence Review, December 8, 1995

FAO Agricultural and Development Economics Division (June 2006). Food Security

FAO, WFP, IFAD. "The State of Food Insecurity in the World 2013. The multiple dimensions of food security."

So I see in your this Mauritius land, you have got enough land to produce food grains. You produce food grain. I understand that instead of growing food grains, you are growing sugar cane for exporting. Why? And you are dependent on food grains, on rice, wheat, dahl. Why? Why this attempt? You first of all grow your own eatables. And if there is time and if your population has got sufficient food grains, then you can try to grow other fruits and vegetables for exporting. The first necessity is that you should be self-sufficient. That is God's arrangement. Everywhere there is sufficient land to produce food grains, not only in your country. I have traveled all over the world -- Africa, Australia, and other, in America also. There are so much land vacant that if we produce food grains, then we can feed ten times as much population as at the present moment. There is no question of scarcity. The whole creation is so made by Krsna that everything is purnam, complete.

~ Srila Prabhupada (Srimad-Bhagavatam 7.5.30 -- Mauritius, October 2, 1975)

7

Soil Change

More Serious Than Climate Change

Earth's climate and biodiversity aren't the only things being dramatically affected by humans—the world's soils are also shifting beneath our feet.

'Global soil change' due to human activities is a major component of what some experts say should be recognized as a new period of geologic time: the human-made age. This new era will be defined by the pervasiveness of human environmental impacts, including changes to Earth's soils and surface geology.

Daniel Richter of Duke University, in his report published in the December 2007 issue of the journal of Soil Science, warns that Earth's soils already show a reduced capacity to support biodiversity and agricultural production. As the amount of depleted and damaged soils increases, global cycles of water, carbon, nitrogen, and other materials are also being affected.

In another paper, Jan Zalaseiwicz of the University of Leicester in England and colleagues argue that the fossil and geologic record

Vasundhara -- a name for mother earth meaning "she who has very fertile soil and unlimited wealth.

of our time will leave distinct signatures that will be apparent far into the future.

Overworked Earth

Today about 50 percent of the world's soils are subject to direct management by humans. Global soil change is also occurring in more remote areas due to the spread of contaminants and alterations in climate. Worldwide, soils are being transformed by human activities in ways that we poorly understand, with possibly dire implications.

The report warns that properties and processes in the soil are more dynamic and susceptible to change than previously thought. Only recently it has been documented that many aspects of soil chemistry and composition are highly responsive to human activities.

Report also warns that severe soil degradation is increasing globally at a rate of 12.4 million to 24.7 million acres (5 million to 10 million hectares) annually.

Soil Degradation And Climate Change - A Relationship

Soil degradation plays much a larger role in climate change than was previously suspected. That's because organic matter in soils store vast amounts of carbon—more than is present in the atmosphere and in all land vegetation combined.

According to the noted geologist Bruce Wilkinson of Syracuse University, heavily cultivated and degraded soils lose their carbon-storing ability as exposed organic matter breaks down.

Over the past half century or so, global soils have lost approximately a hundred billion tons of carbon [in the form of carbon dioxide] to the atmosphere through such exposure. Humans are now the predominant geological force operating on the planet.

Rates of sedimentation and erosion caused by human activities—mainly industrial agriculture—are ten times higher those attributable to natural processes. On agricultural land, soil is being lost ten times faster than it is being replaced. Humans are rapidly consuming the global soil reservoir. In light of the wasting grains to produce meat and biofuels, this is obviously a very serious change.

Reference

FAO (2003). "The State of Food Security in the World 2003"

Eswaran, H.; R. Lal and P.F. Reich. (2001). "Land degradation: an overview"

Ian Sample (2007-08-31). "Global food crisis looms as climate change and population growth strip fertile land"

The environmental crisis is a crisis of values. You can only care deeply if you see the bigger picture. The environment is a mess because we're conditioned to see the earth and its creatures as things to be exploited unlimitedly for personal gratification. We don't treat members of our family like this. Unfortunately, we have forgotten our connection with God.

It's a fact that environmental destruction is due to overindulgence. The uneven distribution of food in the world is due not to food shortages but mainly to greed. Much too much land is being exploited for cash crops-junk foods, exports, tobacco, alcohol. Agribusiness is destroying small farms, food prices are soaring, and soil and forests are disappearing fast. Food has to be returned to the hands of the people.

~ Divine Nature - 7.6, People Working for Change

8

Agrochemical Degeneration Of Land

The use of chemical fertilizers can reduce the natural nutrients on the soil surface. (Fred, 1991) Microorganisms decrease with the continued usage of the chemical fertilizers. (Katsunori, 2003) Chemical fertilizers are regarded as a non-point-source pollution for the environment. Because agriculture is heavily depended on the environmental resources, direct impacts are felt by local farmers with the loss of their ecological systems. (LIU Yu, et al., 2009)

Interestingly, if farmers apply chemical fertilizers or pesticides on their farms day in day out, this results in reduced pest control. Harmful organisms become resistant and beneficial organisms which play a vital role in the improvement of the soil quality will decline. This also leads to land degradation. (Fred, 1991)

The chemical fertilizers used must annihilate both pests and other beneficial organisms that contribute high value functions in agricultural areas. (Preap, 2009)

Chemicals applied to soil take a heavy toll on earthworm which plays a vital role in maintaining soil fertility. (Richard, 2010)

According to Pierre A. Roger and Ian Simpson, 1991, chemical fertilizers are the greatest source of soil degradation and human activities are outweighing natural forces in degrading land resources.

Soil performs many important functions in the upkeep of the natural environment. It not only produces food but also acts as a carbon-sink, reducing the atmospheric pollution, protecting natural resource cycles and recovering nutrients. Chemical fertilizers and pesticides negatively impact soil's ability to perform these functions. (Sununtar, 2006)

Chemical fertilizers, by increasing the abundance of the crops without replacing all the exhausted elements of the soil, have indirectly contributed to change the nutritive value of cereal grains and vegetables.

India - A Case Study

India is the second largest consumption in the world after China, consuming about 26.5 million tonnes. It accounted for 15.3 % of the world's N consumption. 19% of phosphatic and 14.4 % of potassic nutrients in 2008(FAI, 2010).

Fertilizer consumption was around 78 thousand tonnes in 1965-66 and it picked up very fast during the late-1960s and 1970s. At the times of onset of green revolution in 1966-67 consumption of fertilizers was about 1 million tonnes. In 1970-71 total fertilizers consumption increased to 2.26 million tonnes which further increased to 12.73 million tonnes in 1991-92.

During 1990s total fertilization consumption fluctuated between 12.15 and 16.8 million tonnes. Total fertilization consumption reached record level of 26.5 million tonnes 2009-10.

By 2020 fertilizer demands in the country is projected to increase to about 41.6 million tones.

Intensity of Fertilizer Use

In India, per hectare consumption of fertilizers has increased from 69.8 kg in 1991-92 to 113.3 kg in 2006-07, at an average rate of 3.3 percent.

On per hectare basis, fertilizer consumption was less than 2 kg during the 1950s and increased to about 5 kg in 1965-66. However, after introduction of green revolution in 1966-67, per hectare fertilizer consumption more than doubled in the next five years from about 7kg in 1966-67 to about 16 kg in 1971-72, which further increased and reached a level of 50kg in mid-1980s.

Average fertilizer consumption on per hectare basis crossed 100kg in 2005-06 and reached a record level of 135 kg in 2009-10. However, per hectare fertilizer consumption fell during 1973-74 and 1974-75 due to oil shock of 1973 when oil prices quadrupled almost overnight.

The next reversal in intensity of fertilizer use came in 1992-93 when government decontrolled phosphatic and potassic fertilizers

Presently human civilization is based on sense gratification, and consequently more and more people are becoming addicted to different types of things. Demoniac civilization is attached to ugra-karma, horrible activities, and big industries are created to satisfy unfathomable lusty desires. Consequently the people are greatly harassed by governmental taxation. The people are irreligious and do not perform the sacrifices recommended in Bhagavad-gita. Yajnad bhavati parjanyah .... when animals and man are sufficiently fed with grains, they become stronger, their hearts become tranquil and their brains peaceful. They can then advance in spiritual life, life's ultimate destination.

~ Srila Prabhupada (Srimad Bhagavatam 5.5.23)

and increased fertilizer prices significantly. The total fertilizer consumption (N+P+K) fell by about 6 per cent from 69.84 kg per hectare to 65.45 kg per hectare.

However, during the last five years, intensity of fertilizer use has increased substantially (53%) from about 88 kg in 2005-06 to135 kg per hectare in 2009-10.

The intensity of fertilizer use varied greatly from about 48 kg per hectare in Rajasthan to as high as 237 kg per hectare in Punjab. The fertilizer use has generally been higher in northern (91.5 kg/ ha average) and southern (85.3 kg/ha average) region and lower in the eastern (44.7kg/ha) and western region (40.7 kg/ha).

This is happening not only in India, but all over the world. The pattern of chemical fertilizer usage is almost similar everywhere. Farms are seeing dramatic rise in chemical fertilizer use and this is degrading the land at an accelerating pace.

Reference

Demand for Fertiliser in India: Determinants and Outlook for 2020, Vijay Paul Sharma, Hrima Thaker

Eswaran, H.; R. Lal and P.F. Reich. (2001). "Land degradation: an overview". Responses to Land Degradation. 2nd International Conference on Land Degradation and Desertification. New Delhi, India: Oxford Press.

D.L. Johnson and L.A. Lewis, Land Degradation:Creation and Destruction, 2nd edition, Rowman and Littlefield, Lanham, Boulder, New York, 2007

9

Global Grain Production

Below 1980's Level of Use

G lobal annual grains output (grains of all kinds, including wheat, corn, barley, millet, rice, etc.) has declined to around 1,900 million tons or less for the past five years, at a time when over 3,000 million tons of grains produced annually is required to ensure that dietary needs are met globally. There is something radically wrong when the total of the world's grains harvested stagnates, or drops.

The picture is even worse on a per-capita basis. For everyone to have decent daily rations, there needs to be well over 14 bushels of grains available in the world food chain per person, on average. But millions are without even their daily bread. For millions, there are fewer than 10 bushels of grain per capita in the food chain.

Production Is Below 1980s Level of Use

An indication of just how low annual grains output is, is that production is below the average utilization level of the 1980s. Today's global grains output of about 1,900 million tons a year, means that annual grains output is dropping below the level of yearly global grains utilization (for direct human consumption, livestock feed, seed, and all other uses) which existed for several years in the 1980s. This means that more and more people don't have the food they need. And whatever stocks of grains were on hand in recent years as carryover from harvest to harvest or reserves for emergencies have been, relatively speaking, wiped out.

Today world grains carryover stocks are at the same absolute levels they were 20 years ago. Stocks have dropped from 460-490 million metric tons in the late 1980s, down to less than 250 million tons projected for year-end 1995—the level of stocks in 1969.

FIGURE 2
World grains production, per capita
metric tons per capita

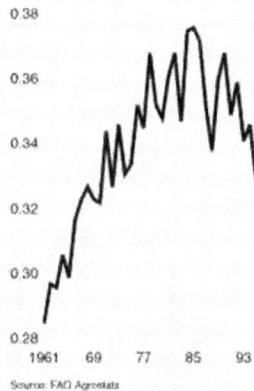

The only reason that there are stocks reported at all is that consumption itself (for livestock feed, cereals consumption, etc.) is declining. This has been apparent for the past few years.

If this grains gap is obvious on the crude scale of world tonnage statistics, it
is even more manifest at the local level, where there are millions of undernourished people at points of need around the globe.

Thus, the situation in grains production and shortages is a good marker of the overall food crisis. Dozens of countries, with millions of people, have gone from national self-sufficiency in basic grains, to dependency on imports or donated cereals aid.

We have seen in India. Nowadays there is no eatables. The government cannot supply food, failure, the problem which is not even amongst the beasts and birds. The birds and beasts, they have no such problem. They are freely living, jumping from one tree to another, because they know there is no problem of eating. And human society, there is problem of eating. What is the advancement? And there is enough place for producing food. I have seen Africa, Australia. Enough place.

~ Srila Prabhupada (Room Conversation with Richard Webster, chairman, Societa Filosofica Italiana -- May 24, 1974, Rome)

Reference

December 8, 1995, Executive Intelligence Review.

Food self-sufficiency rate fell below 40% in 2010 , Japan Times, Aug. 12, 2011

"The Food Bubble Economy". I-sis.org.uk. April 12, 2002.

We're Dead

Without Good Soil

B ad soil is bad for global health, and the evidence is mounting
that the world' soil is in trouble. We're dead without good
soil. Soil holds minerals and organic compounds critical to life.
Without good soil we have got nothing.

The same process of soil degradation which destroyed civilizations
in the past are still at work today. Firstly, billions of tons of soil are
being physically lost each year through accelerated erosion from

the action of water and wind and by undesirable changes in soil structure.

Secondly, many soils are being degraded by increases in their salt content, by waterlogging, or by pollution through the indiscriminate application of chemical and industrial wastes.

Thirdly, many soils are losing the minerals and organic matter that make them fertile, and in most cases, these materials are not being replaced nearly as fast as they are being depleted.

Finally, millions of hectares of good farmland are being lost each year to nonfarm purposes; they are being flooded for reservoirs or paved over for highways, airports, and parking lots. The result of all this mismanagement will be less productive agricultural land at a time when meat consumption is growing and expectations are rising among people everywhere for a better life.

Reference:

Soil erosion: its causes and cures, FAO Corporate Document Repository, Natural Resources Management and Environment Department.

Johnson, Douglas; Lewis, Lawrence. (2007), Land Degradation; Creation and Destruction, Maryland, USA.

"Earth provides enough to satisfy every man's needs, but not every man's greed."
~Mahatma Gandhi

Africa

May Be Able To Feed Only 25% Of Its Population By 2025

According to the experts present at an United Nations University (UNU) conference on desertification in Algiers, Africa may be able to feed just 25% of its population by 2025 if soil degradation on the continent continues at its current pace.

Karl Harmsen, Director of UNU's Ghana-based Institute for Natural Resources in Africa, said that should soil conditions continue to decline in Africa, nearly 75% of the continent could come to rely on some sort of food aid by 2025.

Harmsen's comments come as some 200 delegates from 25 countries convened in Algiers to discuss the causes and consequences of desertification, a threat that puts an estimated 2 billion people at risk of becoming "environmental refugees". The U.N. warns that climate change could worsen the situation by depriving populations living in arid regions of adequate water supplies. Christian

Aid has estimated that an average global temperature increase exceeding 3°C could cause 182 million deaths in Africa this century and leave 750 million additional hungry people in Africa and Asia.

Thus looming desertification could spawn millions of environmental refugees

Reference

Africa Review Report on Drought and Desertification, United Nations Economic And Social Council, Fifth Meeting of the Africa Committee on Sustainable Development, Addis Ababa 22-25 October 2007.

Actually, nobody is dying out of starvation, nobody, not even an animal, not even a bird, dying of starvation, not a beast. God is supplying everyone's food. The problem is with our mismanagement. Food problem exists only in human society. Eko bahunam vidadhati kaman. He is supplying food to the elephant. In Africa there are millions of elephants. They take food, at a time, forty kilos. But they are also being supplied with food. But who is supplying food? We have not arranged food for the elephants, or we have not arranged any food for the ant within our room, but they are being fed by the laws of nature, by God's arrangement. So that is not question. This is our false, I mean to say, idea, that "We shall die out of starvation if we do not make economic condition better." You do it, but you must know that food is already there.

As soon as you take your birth, the food is there. For example, when a child takes birth, a young girl gives birth, just a moment before the birth of the child, there is no milk in the breast, but as soon as the child takes birth, immediately immense supply of milk. So who makes this arrangement? There is already arrangement. Problem is with our mismanagement.

~ Srila Prabhupada (Bhagavad-gita 13.2 -- Melbourne, April 4, 1972)

12

Soil Replenishment

And Survival of Civilization

The history of preceding civilizations and cultures indicate the imbalances that have developed when minerals have been permanently transferred from the soil. There are only a few localities in the world where great civilizations have continued to exist through long periods and these have very distinct characteristics.

It required only a few centuries, and in some profligated systems a few decades to produce so serious a mineral depletion of the soil that progressive plant and animal deterioration resulted. In such instances, regular and adequate replenishment was not taking place.

In nature's program, minerals are loaned temporarily to the plants and animals and their return to the soil is essential. In the case of a forest system, this replenishment is made by its plant and animal life automatically. But in case of agriculture, we have to make a conscious effort to do it. A few intelligent civilizations have done it but the balance of the cultures have largely failed at this point.

Reference

Weston A. Price, Nutrition andPhysical Degeneration, A Comparison of Primitive and Modern Diets and Their Effects, Paul B. Hoeber, Inc, 1939

Starving Billion

A Scandal For Humanity

According to the United Nations, around 950 million people are malnourished or starving in the world today and 1.1 billion people do not have access to safe drinking water.

Attention of mankind has been diverted from necessities to luxuries. There are millions of products like cars, computers, ipods, aeroplanes, TV channels, luxury yatchs, Caribbean vacations, palatial homes, video phones, designer clothes, designer drugs, cosmetic surgery and so on which are vying for our attention, at the cost of the basic necessities. In US, only 1% of population is engaged in agriculture.

Agriculture everywhere else is also a much neglected affair. The result is a global food crisis.

Food Crisis Looms Over 33 Nations

Thirty-three countries, mainly in Africa and Asia, are experiencing 'very serious' to 'grave' food supply problems. The German food relief group Welthungerhilfe and the International Food Policy Research Institute (IFPRI) have warned against neglecting the fate of starving people amidst the current financial crisis.

There is something called annual Global Hunger Index (GHI) which is prepared by the two aforesaid organizations. The GHI

Our first problem is, because we have got this material body, eating. Everyone must eat. So Krsna says in the Bhagavad-gita, annad bhavanti bhutani: [Bg. 3.14] "If there is sufficient food grains, then both man and animal, they become happy." Therefore our first religion is to produce food grain sufficiently to feed everyone. Krsi-go-raksya-vanijyam vaisya-karma svabhava [Bg. 18.44]. This matter has been entrusted to the vaisyas. They should produce sufficient food and give protection to the cows for sufficient milk. Then the whole human society, animal society, will be happy. But we are disobeying the orders or the rules given by God. Instead of producing food, we are producing motorcars. And motor tires, motor parts. And so many other things. And therefore people are starving. The manual labor is being misused. We are disobeying the orders of God. Therefore we are unhappy. I have seen all over the world. There are enough space for producing food grains. And if we actually produce food grain, we can maintain ten times of the present population of the whole world. There is no question of scarcity because God has created everything complete. Purnam idam purnam adaya purnat purnam udacyate [Isopanisad, Invocation]. There cannot be any defect in the creation of God. We have created these defects on account of our disobeying the orders of God. God never said that "motorcar-ad bhavanti bhutani." He never says. But instead of producing food grains, we are producing so many unwanted things. People's energy is engaged for... Just like in America or in every country, so much energy and resources are engaged for preparing war materials. And that means there must be war. And you must be killed; I must be killed. You will kill me; I will kill you. That's all.

~ Srila Prabhupada (Room Conversation with Psychologists from the University of Georgia, March 1, 1975, Atlanta)

index lists 88 countries' food supply situation, with 33 countries chiefly from Asia and Africa in the lower positions. The country with the gravest food situation is Congo.

In view of the current financial crisis, it will be very difficult to mobilise long-term investments required for the urgently needed expansion of agriculture in developing countries. Current financial crisis is a very bad news for the world's hungry.

The GHI index is a compilation based on three chief criteria including the share of undernourished in the population, the number of children below the age of five who are underweight, and the mortality rate for children under five.

Reference

Perez-Escamilla, Rafael; Segall-Correa, Ana Maria (2008). "Food insecurity measurement and indicators"

Conference on Water Scarcity in Africa: Issues and Challenges". Retrieved 18 March 2013.

USAID – Food Security

14

Universe of Soil

Teeming With Life

Soil is comprised of countless species that create a dynamic and complex ecosystem and is among the most precious resources to humans.

All soil is full of life, and good soils are teeming with it. Plants and animals help keep the soil fertile. Plant roots tunnel through the

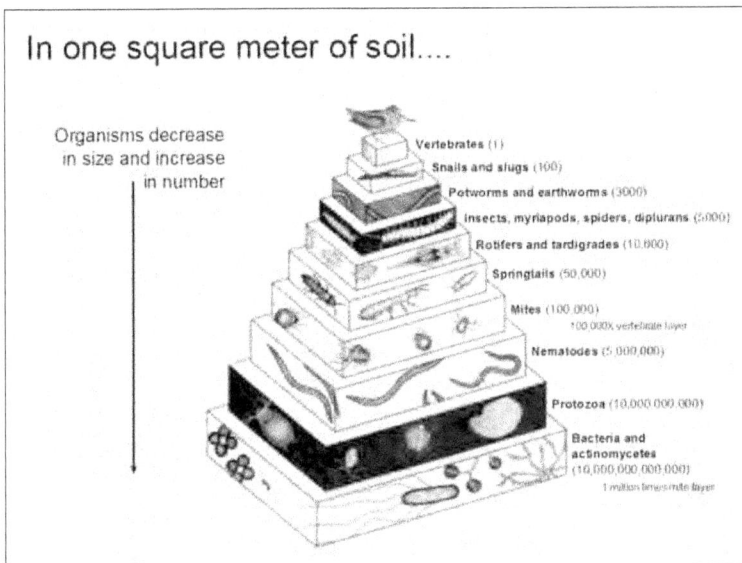

In one square meter of soil....

Organisms decrease in size and increase in number

Vertebrates (1)
Snails and slugs (100)
Potworms and earthworms (3000)
Insects, myriapods, spiders, diplurans (5000)
Rotifers and tardigrades (10,000)
Springtails (50,000)
Mites (100,000)
100,000x vertebrate layer
Nematodes (5,000,000)
Protozoa (10,000,000,000)
Bacteria and actinomycetes (10,000,000,000,000)
1 million times mite layer

soil and break it up, and decaying plants form humus. Burrowing animals mix the soil; the excrete of animals contribute nutrients and improve soil structure.

Besides the soil's more obvious inhabitants, which include rodents, insects, mites, slugs and snails, spiders, and earthworms, there are countless microscopic residents, some helpful to man and his crops, some harmful.

Good soils seem to hold the greatest populations of bacteria. Almost without exception, bacteria are involved in basic enzyme transformations that make possible the growth of higher plants, including our food crops. From man's point of view, bacteria may well be the most valuable of the life forms in soil.

Chemical reactions occur in the soil as a result of exchange of positive ions, or cations. More exchanges take place in clay soils than in any other type. These chemical reactions are also essential to plant growth and development and are a good index of soil fertility.

Reference

World Wildlife Fund, Soil Erosion And Degradation

Vanishing Topsoil Threatens Sustainability of Human Life on Earth, June 2008, David Gutierrez

When tillage begins, other arts follow. The farmers, therefore, are the founders of human civilization.
- Daniel Webster

15

Modern Agriculture

Treating Soil Like Dirt

Since the Industrial Revolution the processes of growth have been speeded up to produce the food and raw materials needed by the population and the factory. Nothing effective has been done to replace the loss of fertility involved in this vast increase in crop and animal production. The consequences have been disastrous.

Half of the topsoil on the planet has been lost in the last 150 years. Agriculture has become unbalanced: the land is in revolt: diseases of all kinds are on the increase: in many parts of the world, nature is removing the worn-out soil by means of erosion.

We are destroying the earth's capital—the soil; we need to be aware of the consequences of this.

The maintenance of the fertility of the soil is the first condition of any permanent system of agriculture. In the ordinary processes of crop production fertility is steadily lost: its continuous restoration by means of manuring and soil management is therefore imperative.

Reference

Sir Albert Howard, An Agricultural Testament, 1940

16

Soil

Deserves Our Love And Care

For thousands of years, farmers took utmost care of their fields. In 1909, American agronomist F.H. King toured China, Korea and Japan, studying traditional fertilization, tillage and general farming practices. He wrote his observations and findings in Farmers of Forty Centuries, Or Permanent Agriculture in China, Korea, and Japan (1911, published shortly after his death by his wife).

> So the mahi, the land, the land is there. Just like in America or in Australia there are so much land. In Africa, so much land lying vacant. But they do not know that this land can produce all the needs of life. Sarva-kama-dugha mahi. Sarva-kama, whatever you want. Actually we are getting... Just like this Western civilization has created so may slaughterhouse for eating purposes. But where from they are getting? From mahi, from the land. If there is no pasturing ground, grazing ground, wherefrom they will get the cows and the bulls? That is also... Because there is grass on the land and the cows and bulls eat them, therefore they grow. Then you cut their throat, civilized man, and eat, you rascal civilized man. But you are getting from the mahi, from the land. Without land, you cannot. Similarly, instead of cutting the throat of the cows, you can grow your food.
> ~ Srila Prabhupada (Lecture, Srimad Bhagavatam 1.10.4, London, November 25, 1973)

King lived in an era preceding synthetic nitrogen fertilizer production and before the use of the internal combustion engine for farm machinery, yet he was profoundly interested in the challenge of farming the same soils in a 'permanent' manner, hence his interest in the agricultural practices of ancient cultures. In recent years, his book became an important organic farming reference.

Reference

Paull, J. (2011) "The making of an agricultural classic: Farmers of Forty Centuries or Permanent Agriculture in China, Korea and Japan, 1911-2011", Agricultural Sciences.

Here mother earth, Dharitri, "O Earth." Earth is being addressed. The whole world is perturbed because the Kali-yuga has begun. Five thousand years ago, when the Kali-yuga began, so all persons were alarmed: "Now the Kali-yuga has begun. So many catastrophes will come in." [SB 1.16.23]

So one instruction is that the earth is addressed, "amba." Amba means mother. So the earth is also our mother. There are seven kinds of mothers. According to sastra, Dharitri, Earth is one of the seven mothers.

atma-mata guroh patni

brahmani raja-patnika

dhenur dhatri tatha prthvi

saptaita matarah smrtah

One's own mother, the wife of the guru, the wife of a brahmana, the wife of a king, the cow, the nurse, and the earth are known as the seven mothers of a man.

~ Srila Prabhupada (Srimad-Bhagavatam 1.16.23 -- Los Angeles, July 13, 1974)

Great Wheat Panic of 2007

In 2007, India's massive purchase of nearly 800,000 tonnes of wheat in the international market at record prices attracted world attention — besides domestic controversy.

This panic purchase added to what agricultural experts are calling the great wheat panic of 2007. Wheat prices had already reached record levels ahead of the Indian move, thanks to falling or stagnating production in many countries — blamed on poor weather and crop diversion. Prices went going through the roof and India's transaction was almost stratospheric.

New Delhi paid $10.64 per bushel compared to the September 2006 price of $4.22 a bushel! For India it was a 'must-buy-to-build-buffer-stock' situation.

$249

$119

This trigger event pushed the world wheat trade into "full-panic mode". Egypt and Iraq followed the deal with large purchases, adding to price pressure

2000

2007

at a time when global stocks were at a 30-year low. India has been an unlikely wheat importer. As the world's second largest wheat producer at around 75 million metric tonne annually (behind

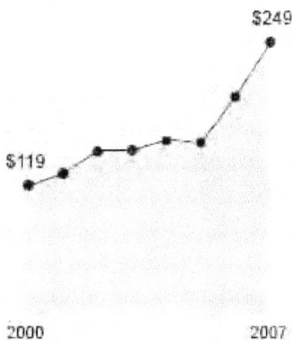

China's 96 million metric tonne), it was widely perceived to be self-sufficient in food production.

Green revolution which took place four decades back is now witnessing diminishing returns as the soil slowly dies from excessive use of chemicals. India's food production stagnated years ago and it is now coming down gradually. One editorial "Panic in wheat" (Business Line, March 20, 2007) noted that "India may well end up with an additional food subsidy of Rs 8,500 crore, including the Rs 3,400 crore spent on the import of 5 million tonnes."

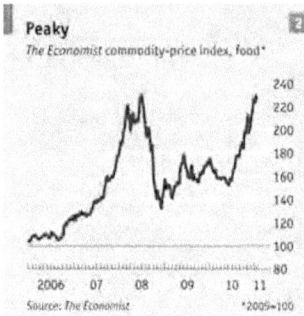

Peaky
The Economist commodity-price index, food*

240
220
200
180
160
140
120
100
80

2006   07   08   09   10   11
Source: The Economist   *2005=100

As a result, major wheat exporters such as US (around 60 million metric tonne annually), Canada and Australia (25 million metric tonne each) have come into play. Coincidentally, all three are major voices in the nuclear suppliers cartel. The wheat crisis, in addition to similar squeeze in food products such as corn and milk in some countries, is so severe that the UN has warned of impending food-related social tensions and political upheaval, leading to social reactions and eventually even political problems."

Also the food prices would continue to rise because of a mix of strong demand from developing countries; a rising global population, more frequent floods and droughts caused by climate change; and the biofuel industry's appetite for grains.

Reference

Chidanand Rajghatta, TNN, Sep 8, 2007, Times of India

Un Warns of Food Price Unrest, Nov 10 2007, Financial Times

World's Land Turning to Desert at Alarming Speed

United Nations Warns

By Chris Hawley, Associated Press, June 16, 2004

UNITED NATIONS -- The world is turning to dust, with lands the size of Rhode Island becoming desert wasteland every year and the problem threatening to send millions of people fleeing to greener countries, the United Nations says.

One-third of the Earth's surface is at risk, driving people into cities and destroying agriculture in vast swaths of Africa. Thirty-one percent of Spain is threatened, while China has lost 36,000 square miles to desert -- an area the size of Indiana -- since the 1950s.

This week the United Nations marks the 10th anniversary of the Convention to Combat Desertification, a plan aimed at stopping the phenomenon. Despite the efforts, the trend seems to be picking up speed -- doubling its pace since the 1970s.

"It's a creeping catastrophe," said Michel Smitall, a spokesman for the U.N. secretariat that oversees the 1994 accord. "Entire parts of the world might become uninhabitable."

Slash-and-burn agriculture, sloppy conservation, overtaxed water supplies and industrialization of agriculture are mostly to blame. But global warming is taking its toll, too.

The United Nations is holding a ceremony in Bonn, Germany, to mark World Day to Combat Desertification, and will hold a meeting in Brazil to take stock of the problem.

The warning comes as a controversial movie, "The Day After Tomorrow" is whipping up interest in climate change, and as rivers and lakes dry up in the American West, giving Americans a taste of what's to come elsewhere.

The United Nations says:

* From the mid-1990s to 2000, 1,374 square miles have turned into deserts each year -- an area about the size of Rhode Island. That's up from 840 square miles in the 1980s, and 624 square miles during the 1970s.

* By 2025, two-thirds of arable land in Africa will disappear, along with one-third of Asia's and one-fifth of South America's.

* Some 135 million people -- equivalent to the populations of France and Germany combined -- are at risk of being displaced.

Most at risk are dry regions on the edges of deserts -- places like sub-Saharan Africa or the Gobi Desert in China, where people are already struggling to eke out a living from the land.

As consumption expands, those regions have become more stressed. Trees are cut for firewood, grasslands are overgrazed, fields are over-farmed and lose their nutrients, water becomes scarcer and dirtier.

Technology can make the problem worse. In parts of Australia, irrigation systems are pumping up salty water and slowly poisoning farms. In Saudi Arabia, herdsmen can use water trucks instead of taking their animals from oasis to oasis -- but by staying in one place, the herds are getting bigger and eating all the grass.

In Spain, Portugal, Italy and Greece, coastal resorts are swallowing up water that once moistened the wilderness. Many farmers in those countries still flood their fields instead of using more miserly "drip irrigation," and the resulting shortages are slowly baking the life out of the land.

The result is a patchy "rash" of dead areas, rather than an easy-to-see expansion of existing deserts, scientists say. These areas have their good times and bad times as the weather changes. But in general, they are getting bigger and worse-off.

"It's not as dramatic as a flood or a big disaster like an earthquake,"

said Richard Thomas of the International Center for Agricultural Research in the Dry Areas in Aleppo, Syria. "There are some bright spots and hot spots. But overall, there is a trend toward increasing degradation."

The trend is speeding up, but it has been going on for centuries, scientists say. Fossilized pollen and seeds, along with ancient tools like grinding stones, show that much of the Middle East, the Mediterranean and North Africa were once green. The Sahara itself was a savanna, and rock paintings show giraffes, elephants and cows once lived there.

Global warming contributes to the problem, making many dry areas drier, scientists say. In the last century, average temperatures have risen over 1 degree Fahrenheit worldwide, according to the U.S. Global Change Research Program.

As for the American Southwest, it is too early to tell whether its six-year drought could turn to something more permanent. But scientists note that reservoir levels are dropping as cities like Phoenix and Las Vegas expand.

"In some respects you may have greener vegetation showing up in people's yards, but you may be using water that was destined for the natural environment," said Stuart Marsh of the University of Arizona's Office of Arid Lands Studies. "That might have an effect on the biodiversity surrounding that city."

The Global Change Research Program says global warming could eventually make the Southwest wetter -- but it will also cause more extreme weather, meaning harsher droughts that could kill vegetation. Now, the

Just like last time I was in Europe, everything is now drying. I'm coming from London, Paris, and Tehran. All fields yellow. And Europe, so much scorching heat and sunshine, I never seen. This time I saw everything has become yellow. Greenness gone.

What scientific method you have got? Bring water. Now they are thinking of bringing, importing water. So this will be the punishment. In the Kali-yuga, as people become godless, this punishment will be there: no water, no food supply. And over and above that, government taxation. You'll be harassed. Three things will go on.

~ Srila Prabhupada (Srimad-Bhagavatam 1.7.25 -- Vrndavana, September 22, 1976)

Southwest drought has become so severe that even the sagebrush is dying.

"The lack of water and the overuse of water, that is going to be a threat to the United States," Thomas said. "In other parts of the world, the problem is poverty that causes people to overuse the land. Most of these ecological systems have tipping points, and once you go past them, things go downhill."

References:
United Nations Convention to Combat Desertification: www.unccd.int
International Center for Agricultural Research in the Dry Areas : www. icarda.org/
University of Arizona Office of Arid Lands Studies: ag.arizona.edu/OALS/ oals/oals.html

38% of World's Land in Danger of Turning into Desert

Brian Merchant, February 10, 2010

And now an analysis of the global desertification threat has revealed that 38% of surfaces around the world are vulnerable.

Science Daily reports:

"Researchers have measured the degradation of the planet's soil using the Life Cycle Assessment (LCA), a scientific methodology that analyses the environmental impact of human activities, and which now for the first time includes indicators on desertification. The results show that 38 percent of the world is made up of arid regions at risk of desertification."

Which is unfortunate news, to say the least. The study divided the world's land into "15 natural areas or "eco-regions" according to their degree of aridity." And 8 of those eco regions--that cover 38% of the planet--were deemed at risk of falling victim to desertification.

According to Science Daily, the 8 areas most prone to turn into desert are:

• coastal areas

- the Prairies
- the Mediterranean region
- the savannah
- the temperate Steppes
- the temperate deserts
- tropical and subtropical Steppes
- the tropical and subtropical deserts

The areas at greatest risk are the subtropical deserts--areas in North Africa, Australia, and the Middle East were determined to have the highest desertification risk factor, a 7.6 out of 10. The Mediterranean region had the next highest risk. And bear in mind that while all of this sounds a little heavy on the doom and gloom side, it's very real: there are estimates that in China, for example, 1300 square miles of desert are created every year.

This sobering news means that an additional emphasis must be placed on land management and careful water conservation, especially in the most at-risk areas--unless we want to see a full third of the planet eventually get swallowed up in desert.

You have seen desert. Desert means it requires huge quantities of water. Nowadays, practically, in every country, especially in India, every land is just like desert for want of water. So you see in Vrndavana so much land lying vacant, no agriculture. Why? There is want of water. There is no sufficient supply of water. So in this way, if there is scarcity of water, then gradually these places will be converted into desert. Converted into desert. So the "desert" word is used because it requires huge quantity of water. Similarly, we are, in this material world, we are trying to be happy in the society, friendship and love. Suta-mita-ramani-samaje. But the happiness we are getting, that is compared with a drop of water in the desert. If in the vast desert, Arabian desert, if we say that "We want water," and somebody brings a drop of water and take it, it will be very insignificant, has no meaning.
~ Srila Prabhupada (Bhagavad-gita 9.1 -- Vrndavana, April 17, 1975)

1

9

Food Riots

The Worst Food Crisis in 45 Years

In 2008, Food riots erupted around the world. Protests occurred in Egypt, Cameroon, the Philippines, Burkina Faso, Ivory Coast, Mauritania and Senegal. One Senegalese demonstrator told new reporters: "We are holding this demonstration because we are hungry. We need to eat, we need to work, we are hungry. That's all. We are hungry." United Nations Secretary-General Ban Ki-moon convened a task force to confront the problem, which threatens, he said, "the specter of widespread hunger, malnutrition and social unrest on an unprecedented scale." The World Food Program called the food crisis the worst in 45 years, dubbing it a "silent tsunami" that would plunge 100 million more people into hunger.

Food riots in Haiti killed six, injured hundreds and led to the ousting of Prime Minister Jacques-Edouard Alexis. One visiting dignitary wrote that, "hunger is on the march here. Garbage is carefully sifted for whatever food might be left. Young babies wail in frustration, seeking milk from a mother too anemic to produce it."

59

There was a global food crisis in 1946. Then, as now, the U.N. convened a working group to deal with it. At its meeting, the head of the U.N. Relief and Rehabilitation Administration, said, "Ticker tape ain't spaghetti." In other words, the stock market doesn't feed the hungry. His words remain true today.

That was being maintained during the time of Maharaja Yudhisthira. That is being described. Maharaja Yudhisthira maintained this standard of civilization. Just see how the economic problems will be solved simply by God consciousness. Try to understand, Mahi, Earth. Because Earth will produce everything. Just like here in this Letchmore Heath there is so much land lying vacant. You produce you own food. Why you are going to London, to the factories? There is no need. This is wrong civilization. Here is land. You produce your food. If you produce your food, there is no need of going hundred miles, fifty miles on your motorcycle or motor to earn your livelihood. Why? There is no need. Then you require petrol. And petrol there is scarcity. Then you require so many parts and so many things means you are making the whole thing complicated unnecessarily. Unnecessarily. There is no need. Simply you keep to the land and produce your food, and the cows are there. They will supply you milk. Then where is your economic problems. If you have sufficient grains, sufficient vegetables, sufficient milk from the land where you are living, where your economic problem? Why you should go to other place? That is Vedic civilization. Everyone should remain in the spot and produce everything as he requires, and God will help you. Because you can produce from the land anywhere. The rainfall is there. If you have got land and the rainfall is regular, then you can produce anything. Kamam vavarsa parjanyah [SB 1.10.4]. And how the rainfall will be possible? How regular rainfall? That is described in the Bhagavata. Yajnad bhavati parjanyah parjanyad anna-sambhavah [Bg. 3.14].

~ Srila Prabhupada (Lecture, Srimad Bhagavatam 1.10.4, London, November 25, 1973)

Reference

Amy Goodman, Breaking the Sound Barrier, P 132-133

Ticker Tape Ain't Spaghetti, May 01, 2008, Amy Goodman, Dennis Moynihan

20

Soil Replenishment

By Annual Overflow of Great River Systems

An important procedure for the replenishing of the depleted soils is by the annual overflow of great river systems which float enrichment from the highlands to the lower plains. This is illustrated by the history of the rivers like the Ganges or the Nile which have carried their generous blanket of fertilizing humus and rich soil over their long course and thus made it possible for the plains to sustain a very dense population. Where human beings have deforested vast mountainsides at the sources of these great waterways, the whole situation has reversed.

For example in China, its two great rivers, the Yangtze and the Yellow River have their source in the isolated vastness of the Himalayas in Tibet and through the centuries have provided the replenishment needed for supporting the vast population of the plains. Because of this natural replenishment, the Chinese have been exceedingly efficient in returning to the soil the minerals borrowed by the plant and animal life. Their efficiency as agriculturists has exceeded that of the residents of many other parts of the world.

But this is no longer so. Under the pressure of industrial progress, more and more of the highlands have been denuded. The forests have been ruthlessly cut down. Vast areas that nature had taken millenniums to forest have been denuded and the soil has been washed away in a few decades. These mountainsides have become a great menace instead of a great storehouse of plant food material for the plains.

The heavy rains now find little impediment and rush madly toward the plains, carrying with them not the rich vegetable matter of the previous era, but clay and rocks. This material is not good. Instead of replenishing the soil, it covers the plains with a layer of silt many feet deep, making it impossible to utilize the fertile soil underneath.

We have only to look over the departed civilizations of historic times to see the wreckage and devastation caused by these processes.

As stated in Isopanisad, this material creation is supplied with all the potencies for the production of all necessities required by the living entities -- not only human beings, but animals, reptiles, aquatics and trees. The oceans and seas produce pearls, coral and valuable jewels so that fortunate law-abiding people can utilize them. Similarly, the hills are full of chemicals so that when rivers flow down from them the chemicals spread over the fields to fertilize the four kinds of foodstuffs. These are technically known as carvya (those edibles which are chewed), lehya (those which are licked up), cusya (those which are sucked) and peya (those which are drunk).

~ Srila Prabhupadas (Srimad Bhagavatam 4.19.9)

The rise and fall in succession of such cultures as those of Greece, Rome, North Africa, Spain, and many districts of Europe, have followed the pattern which we are now pursuing with great pride, under the illusion of progress.

The complacency with which the mass of the people as well as the politicians view this trend is not unlike the drifting of a merry party in the rapids over a great water fall. There seems to be no sense of impending doom.

It is apparent that the present and past one or two generations have taken more than their share of the minerals and have done so without duly returning them back. Thus they have handicapped, to a serious extent, the succeeding generations. It is not easy to replenish the minerals in the soil and it practically takes many centuries to accumulate another layer of topsoil.

This constitutes one of the serious dilemmas. A program that does not include maintaining this balance between population and soil productivity must inevitably lead to disastrous degeneration. Over-population means strife and wars.

The history of many civilizations has recorded a progressive rise while civilizations were using the accumulated nutrition in the topsoil, and a progressive decline when these civilizations were destroying these essential sources of life. Their cycle of rise and fall is strikingly duplicated in our present industrial culture.

By God's arrangement one can have enough food grains, enough milk, enough fruits and vegetables, and nice clear river water. But now I have seen, while traveling in Europe, that all the rivers there have become nasty. In Germany, in France, and also in Russia and America I have seen that the rivers are nasty. By nature's way the water in the ocean is kept clear like crystal, and the same water is transferred to the rivers, but without salt, so that one may take nice water from the river. This is nature's way, and nature's way means Krsna's way.

~ Srila Prabhupada (Teachings of Queen Kunti 23)

Reference

Weston A. Price, Nutrition and Physical Degeneration, A Comparison of Primitive and Modern Diets and Their Effects, Paul B. Hoeber, Inc, New York, 1939

PRICE, W. A. New light on the control of dental caries and the degenerative diseases. J. Am. Dent. Assn., 18:1889, 1931.

ORR, J. B. The composition of the pasture. London, H. M. Stationery Office. E.M.B., 18, 1929.

21

Profiteers Squeeze Billions

Out of Growing Global Food Crisis

G iant agribusinesses are enjoying soaring earnings and profits out of the world food crisis which is driving millions of people towards starvation and speculation is helping to drive the prices of basic foodstuffs out of the reach of the hungry.

The prices of wheat, corn and rice soared in 2008 driving the world's poor -- who already spend about 80 per cent of their income on food -- into hunger and destitution.

The World Bank says that 100 million more people are facing severe hunger. Yet some of the world's richest food companies are making record profits. Monsanto reported that its net income for the three months up to the end of February 2008 had more than doubled over the same period in 2007, from $543m (£275m) to $1.12 billion. Its profits increased from $1.44 billion to $2.22 billion.

Cargill's net earnings soared by 86 per cent from $553m to $1.030 billion over the same three months. And Archer Daniels Midland, one of the world's largest agricultural processors of soy, corn and wheat, increased its net earnings by 42 per cent in the first three months of 2008 from \$363m to \$517m. The operating profit of its grains

merchandising and handling operations jumped 16-fold from \$21m to \$341m.

Similarly, the Mosaic Company, one of the world's largest fertilizer companies, saw its income for the three months

"You can illustrate our financial report with nudie photos, but it's not the same thing as obscene profits."

ending 29 February 2008 rise more than 12-fold, from \$42.2m to \$520.8m, on the back of a shortage of fertiliser. The prices of some kinds of fertiliser have more than tripled over the past year as demand has outstripped supply. As a result, plans to increase harvests in developing countries have been hit hard.

The Food and Agriculture Organisation reports that 37 developing countries are in urgent need of food. And food riots are

breaking out across the globe from Bangladesh to Burkina Faso, from China to Cameroon, and from Uzbekistan to the United Arab Emirates.

Benedict Southworth, director of the World Development Movement, called the escalating earnings and profits "immoral". He said that the benefits of the food price increases were being kept by the big companies, and were not finding their way down to farmers in the developing world.

The soaring prices of food and fertilisers partly come from increasing appetites for meat, especially in India and China;

producing 1 pound of beef for example, takes 21 pounds of grain. World food stocks at record lows, export bans and a drought in Australia have contributed to the crisis, but experts are also fingering food speculation.

Reference

Geoffrey Lean, Multinationals Make Billions In Profit Out of Growing Global Food Crisis, May 04, 2008, The Independent/UK

Trade is meant only for transporting surplus produce to places where the produce is scanty. But when traders become too greedy and materialistic they take to large-scale commerce and industry and allure the poor agriculturalist to unsanitary industrial towns with a false hope of earning more money. The industrialist and the capitalist do not want the farmer to remain at home, satisfied with his agricultural produce. When the farmers are satisfied by a luxuriant growth of food grains, the capitalist becomes gloomy at heart. But the real fact is that humanity must depend on agriculture and subsist on agricultural produce.

No one can produce rice and wheat in big iron factories. The industrialist goes to the villagers to purchase the food grains he is unable to produce in his factory. The poor agriculturalist takes advances from the capitalist and sells his produce at a lower price. Hence when food grains are produced abundantly the farmers become financially stronger, and thus the capitalist becomes morose at being unable to exploit them.

~ Srila Prabhupada (Light of Bhagavata, verse 9)

Growth And Decay

The Wheel of Life

By Sir Albert Howard, 1940

The wheel of life is made up of two processes—growth and decay. The one is the counterpart of the other. The processes of decay which round off and complete the wheel of life can be seen in operation on the floor of any woodland. It can be seen how the mixed animal and vegetable wastes are converted into humus and how the forest manures itself.

Such are the essential facts in the wheel of life. Growth on the one side: decay on the other. In Nature's farming a balance is struck and maintained between these two complementary processes.

The only man-made systems of agriculture—those to be found in the East—which have stood the test of time have faithfully copied this rule in Nature. It follows therefore that the correct relation between the processes of growth and the processes of decay is the first principle of successful farming. Agriculture must always be balanced. If we speed up growth we must accelerate decay. If, on the other hand, the soil's reserves are squandered, crop production ceases to be good farming: it becomes something very different.

The farmer is transformed into a bandit.

Reference

Sir Albert Howard, An Agricultural Testament, 1940

World Cupboard

Has 57 Days Supply of Grains

Whenever there is a shortfall in the amount of food produced in any given year, it is possible to dip into an international cupboard or reserve of grains (wheat, rice and corn, for example) left over from previous years of good harvests. Tabs have been kept on the size of that reserve by the U.S. Department of Agriculture since the end of World War II but recent figures revealed that the international cupboard or "reserve" of grains (wheat, rice and corn, for example), is now at its lowest point since the early

1970s. This is the outcome of a nasty agriculture policy which is all about finding ways to raise prices by getting rid of farm surpluses and not about feeding people.

The world's grain reserves are now at its lowest point since the early 1970s. There is enough in the cupboard to keep people alive on basic grains for 57 days. Two months of survival foods is all that separates mass starvation from drought, plagues of locusts and other pests, or wars and violence that disrupt farming, all of which are more plentiful than food.

To put the 57 days in historical perspective, the world price for wheat went up six-fold in 1973, the last time reserves were this low. Then there are two other pressing demands for grains that were not as forceful during the 1970s, feedstock for ethanol and livestock feed. Wealthy nations are converting grains into fuel and meat while others are starving.

Historians will also recall that 1970s food prices went up alongside price hikes for oil, contributing to the runaway inflation that defined the

Mostly people, they have no provision for eating either today or tomorrow. Manda-bhagya. There is no sufficient grains. Formerly even in the villages you would see that a common man has very good stock of foodgrains and cows, dhanvena dhanavan, gavaya dhanavan. Formerly the standard of richness was considered how many morai, what is called? Where grain is stocked? Silo. So in India it is called morai, grain stock. And how many cows one has got in stock. Then he is a rich man. Nowadays how much paper money he has got. Actually it has no value. Suppose you have got some papers. Each paper it is written there "one thousand dollars." But if there is no grain, what will this one-thousand-dollars paper will do? It actually so happened in the last war in Germany. Their money was thrown in the street. Nobody cared to take it, because it has no exchange. So long the paper money you can exchange, there is value. Otherwise it is paper only. But if you have got actual commodity -- grains and cows -- then you can eat in any circumstances.

~ Srila Prabhupada (Srimad-Bhagavatam 5.5.3 -- Vrndavana, October 25, 1976)

decade's economic challenge. The 1970s experience shows that seemingly small blips in food reserves and availability can lead to major shocks in the economy and society.

Even modest price changes can carry a big wallop especially in a world that is already suffering from crisis-overload. For a third of the world is people who subsist on less than two dollars a day, pennies can make a life and death difference. A garden on top of every garage, a veggie stew in every pot, we might see this and more in the years ahead.

Source

Wayne Roberts , Grain Drain: Get Ready for Peak Grain, Oct 31 2006, Energy Bulletin,

24

Nature's Methods

Of Soil Management

By Sir Albert Howard, 1940

L ittle or no consideration is paid in the literature of agriculture to the means by which Nature manages land and conducts her water culture. Nevertheless, these natural methods of soil management must form the basis of all our studies of soil fertility.

What are the main principles underlying Nature's agriculture? These can most easily be seen in operation in our woods and forests. Mixed farming is the rule: plants are always found with animals: many species of plants and animals all live together. In the forest every form of animal life, from mammals to the simplest invertebrates, occurs. The vegetable kingdom exhibits a similar range: there is never any attempt at monoculture: mixed crops and mixed farming are the rule.

The soil is always protected from the direct action of sun, rain, and wind. In this care of the soil strict economy is the watchword: nothing is lost. The whole of the energy of sunlight is made use of by the foliage of the forest canopy and of the undergrowth. The leaves also break up the rainfall into fine spray so that it can the more easily be dealt with by the litter of plant and animal remains which provide the last line of defence of the precious soil. These methods of protection, so effective in dealing with sun and rain, also reduce the power of the strongest winds to a gentle air current.

The rainfall in particular is carefully conserved. A large portion is retained in the surface soil: the excess is gently transferred to the subsoil and in due course to the streams and rivers. The fine spray created by the foliage is transformed by the protective ground litter into thin films of water which move slowly downwards, first into the humus layer and then into the soil and subsoil. These latter have been made porous in two ways: by the creation of a wellmarked crumb structure and by a network of drainage and aeration channels made by earthworms and other burrowing animals. The pore space of the forest soil is at its maximum so that there is a large internal soil surface over which the thin films of water can creep.

There is also ample humus for the direct absorption of moisture. The excess drains away slowly by way of the subsoil. There is remarkably little run-off, even from the primeval rain forest. When this occurs it is practically clear water. Hardly any soil is removed.

Nothing in the nature of soil erosion occurs. The streams and rivers in forest areas are always perennial because of the vast quantity of water in slow transit between the rainstorms and the sea. There is therefore little or no drought in forest areas because so much of the rainfall is retained exactly where it is needed. There is no waste anywhere.

The forest manures itself. It makes its own humus and supplies itself with minerals. If we watch a piece of woodland we find that

mayadhyaksena prakrtih
suyate sa-caracaram
hetunanena kaunteya
jagad viparivartate
This material nature, which is one of My energies, is working under My direction, O son of Kunti, producing all moving and nonmoving beings. Under its rule this manifestation is created and annihilated again and again.
~ *Bhagavad-gita 9.10*

a gentle accumulation of mixed vegetable and animal residues is constantly taking place on the ground and that these wastes are being converted by fungi and bacteria into humus. The processes involved in the early stages of this transformation depend throughout on oxidation: afterwards they take place in the absence of air. They are sanitary. There is no nuisance of any kind—no smell, no flies, no dustbins, no incinerators, no artificial sewage system, no water-borne diseases, no town councils, and no rates. On the contrary, the forest affords a place for the ideal summer holiday: sufficient shade and an abundance of pure fresh air.

The mineral matter needed by the trees and the undergrowth is obtained from the subsoil. This is collected in dilute solution in water by the deeper roots, which also help in anchoring the trees.

Even in soils markedly deficient in phosphorus trees have no difficulty in obtaining ample supplies of this element. Potash, phosphate, and other minerals are always collected in situ and carried by the transpiration current for use in the green leaves.

Afterwards they are either used in growth or deposited on the floor of the forest in the form of vegetable waste—one of the constituents needed in the synthesis of humus. This humus is again utilized by the roots of the trees. Nature's farming, as seen in the forest, is characterized by two things: (1) a constant circulation of the mineral matter absorbed by the trees; (2) a constant addition of new mineral matter from the vast reserves held in the subsoil. There is therefore no need to add phosphates: there is no necessity for more potash salts. No mineral deficiencies of any kind occur. The supply of all the manure needed is automatic and is provided either by humus or by the soil. There is a natural division of the subject into organic and inorganic. Humus provides the organic manure: the soil the mineral matter.

The soil always carries a large fertility reserve. There is no hand to mouth existence about Nature's farming. The reserves are carried in the upper layers of the soil in the form of humus. Yet any useless accumulation of humus is avoided because it is automatically mingled with the upper soil by the activities of burrowing animals such as earthworms and insects.

The extent of this enormous reserve is only realized when the trees are cut down and the virgin land is used for agriculture. When plants like tea, coffee, rubber, and bananas are grown on recently cleared land, good crops can be raised without manure for ten years or more. Like all good administrators, therefore, Nature carries strong liquid reserves effectively invested. There is no squandering of these reserves to be seen anywhere.

The crops and live stock look after themselves. Nature has never found it necessary to design the equivalent of the spraying machine and the poison spray for the control of insect and fungous pests. There is nothing in the nature of vaccines and serums for the protection of the live stock. It is true that all kinds of diseases are to be found here and there among the plants and animals of the forest, but these never assume large proportions. The principle followed is that the plants and animals can very well protect themselves even when such things as parasites are to be found in their midst. Nature's rule in these matters is to live and let live.

Therefore, the supreme will is behind all cosmic activities. Of course, there are atheists of various categories who do not believe in a creator, but that is due to a poor fund of knowledge. The modern scientist, for example, has created space satellites, and by some arrangement or other, these satellites are thrown into outer space to fly for some time at the control of the scientist who is far away. Similarly, all the universes with innumerable stars and planets are controlled by the intelligence of the Personality of Godhead.

~ Srila Prabhupada (Srimad Bhagavatam 1.1.1)

If we study the prairie and the ocean we find that similar principles are followed. The grass carpet deals with the rainfall very much as the forest does. There is little or no soil erosion: the run-off is practically clear water. Humus is again stored in the upper soil.

The best of the grassland areas of North America carried a mixed herbage which maintained vast herds of bison. No veterinary service was in existence for keeping these animals alive. When brought into cultivation by the early settlers, so great was the store of fertility that these prairie soils yielded heavy crops of wheat for many years without live stock and without manure.

In lakes, rivers, and the sea, mixed farming is again the rule: a great variety of plants and animals are found living together: nowhere does one find monoculture. The vegetable and animal wastes are again dealt with by effective methods. Nothing is wasted. Humus again plays an important part and is found everywhere in solution, in suspension, and in the deposits of mud. The sea, like the forest and the prairie, manures itself.

The main characteristic of Nature's farming can therefore be summed up in a few words. *Mother earth never attempts to farm without livestock;* she always raises mixed crops; great pains are taken to preserve the soil and to prevent erosion; the mixed vegetable and animal wastes are converted into humus; there is no waste; the processes of growth and the processes of decay balance one another; ample provision is made to maintain large reserves of fertility; the greatest care is taken to store the rainfall; both plaints and animals are left to protect themselves against disease.

In considering the various man-made systems of agriculture, which so far have been devised, it will be interesting to see how far Nature's principles have been adopted, whether they have ever been improved upon, and what happens when they are disregarded.

Source
An Agricultural Testament, 1940

25

Agricultural Meltdown

The Last Straw That Would Break The Civilization's Back

Agriculture is our last frontier to get destroyed. The oil is going. Finances are in dire straits. Agriculture is next meltdown and looks like it is ripe.

UN Food and Agriculture Organization (FAO) Director-General Jacques Diouf has called on US President Barack Obama to make the eradication of world hunger a priority on his agenda and to host a world summit on the issue in the first half of this year.

In a message congratulating Obama on his election, Diouf said the US should, "in the first semester of 2009, take a leadership role in convening a World Summit on Food Security in order to reach a wide and common consensus on the definitive elimination of hunger from the world."

Heightened awareness of the plight of 923 million hungry persons as a result of the ongoing global food and financial crises created a "special window of opportunity for such an initiative," he added. FAO pointed out that the surge in food prices over the past year has increased the number of undernourished people in the world to an estimated 923 million, and this number could grow.

Reference

UN News Service, Nov 7, 2008

Peter Salonius, Agriculture: Unsustainable Resource Depletion, October, 2008

Driving at breakneck speed. And then what is the business? Searching out some means of food, exactly like the hog, he is loitering here and there, "Where is stool? Where is stool? Where is stool?" And this is going on in the polished way as civilization. There is so much risk, as running these cars so many people are dying. There is record, it is very dangerous. At least I feel as soon as I go to the street, it is dangerous. The motorcar are running so speedy, and what is the business? The business is where to find out food. So therefore it is condemned that this kind of civilization is hoggish civilization. This hog is running after, "Where is stool? And you are running in a car. Purpose is the same: Therefore this is not advancement of civilization. Advancement of civilization is, as Krsna advises, that you require food, so produce food grain. Remain wherever you are. You can produce food grain anywhere, a little labor. And keep cows, go-raksya, krsi-go-raksya vanijyam vaisya-karma svabhava-jam [Bg. 18.44]. Solve your problem like... Produce your food wherever you are there. Till little, little labor, and you will get your whole year's food. And distribute the food to the animals, cows, and eat yourself. The cow will eat the refuse. You take the rice, and the skin you give to the cow. From dahl you take the grain, and the skin you give to the... And fruit, you take the fruit, and the skin you give to the cow, and he will give you milk. So why should you kill her? Milk is the miraculous food; therefore Krsna says cow protection. Give protection to the cow, take milk from it, and eat food grains -- your food problem is solved. Where is food problem? Why should you invent such civilization always full of anxieties, running the car here and there, and fight with other nation, and economic development? What is this civilization?

~Srila Prabhupada (Philosophical discussion)

26

The Agriculture Of The Nations

Which Have Passed Away

By Sir Albert Howard, 1940

The difficulties inherent in the study of the agriculture of the nations which are no more are obvious. Unlike their buildings, where it is possible from a critical study of the buried remains of cities to reproduce a picture of bygone civilizations, the fields of the ancients have seldom been maintained. The land has either gone back to forest or has been used for one system of farming after another.

Peruvian Legacy

In one case, however, the actual fields of a bygone people have been preserved together with the irrigation methods by which these lands were made productive. No written records, alas, have come down to us of the staircase cultivation of the ancient Peruvians, perhaps one of the oldest forms of Stone Age agriculture.

This arose either in mountains or in the upland areas under grass because of the difficulty, before the discovery of iron, of removing the dense forest growth. In Peru irrigated staircase farming seems to have reached its highest known development. The National Geographical Society of the United States sent an expedition to study the relics of this ancient method of agriculture, an account of which was published by O. F. Cook in the Society's Magazine of May 1916, under the title: 'Staircase Farms of the Ancients.'

The system of the megalithic people of old Peru was to construct a stairway of terraced fields up the slopes of the mountains, tier upon tier, sometimes as many as fifty in number. The outer retaining walls of these terraces were made of large stones which fit into one another with such accuracy that even at the present day, like those of the Egyptian pyramids, a knife blade cannot be inserted between them.

After the retaining wall was built, the foundation of the future field was prepared by means of coarse stones covered with clay. On this basis layers of soil, several feet thick, originally imported from beyond the great mountains, were super-imposed and then levelled for irrigation. The final result was a small flat field with only just sufficient slope for artificial watering.

In other words, a series of huge flower pots, each provided with ample drainage below, was prepared with incredible labour by this ancient people for their crops. Such were the megalithic achievements in agriculture, beside which 'our undertakings sink into insignificance in face of what this vanished race accomplished. The narrow floors and steep walls of rocky valleys that would appear utterly worthless and hopeless to our engineers were transformed, literally made over, into fertile lands and were the homes of teeming populations in pre-historic days' (O. F. Cook).

The engineers of old Peru did what they did through necessity because iron, steel, reinforced concrete, and the modern power units

had not been invented. The plunder of the forest soil was beyond their reach.

These terraced fields had to be irrigated. Water had to be led to them over immense distances by means of aqueducts. Prescott states that one which traversed the district of Condesuyu measured between four and five hundred miles. Cook gives a photograph of one of these channels as a thin dark line traversing a steep mountain wall many hundreds of feet above the valley.

Modern Day Semblance

These ancient methods of agriculture are represented at the present day by the terraced cultivation of the Himalayas, of the mountainous areas of China and Japan, and of the irrigated rice fields so common in the hills of South India, Ceylon, and the Malayan Archipelago.

Conway's description, published in 1894, of the terraces of Hunza on the North-West Frontier of India and of the canal, carried for long distances across the face of precipices to the one available supply of perennial water—the torrent from the Ultor glacier—tallies almost completely with what he found in 1901 in the Bolivian Andes.

This distinguished scholar and mountaineer considered that the native population of Hunza of the present day is living in a stage of

If your energy is all engaged in manufacturing tires and wheels, then who will go to the... Actually I have seen in your country. Now the farmers' son, they do not like to remain in the farm. They go in the city. I have seen it. The farmers' son, they do not like to take up the profession of his father. So gradually farming will be reduced, and the city residents, they are satisfied if they can eat meat. And the farmer means keeping the, raising the cattle and killing them, send to the city, and they will think that "We are eating. What is the use of going to..." But these rascals have no brain that "If there is no food grain or grass, how these cattle will be...?" Actually it is happening. They are eating swiftly.

-Srila Prabhupada (Room Conversation with Dr. Theodore Kneupper — November 6, 1976, Vrndavana)

civilization that must bear no little likeness to that of the Peruvians under Inca government. An example of this ancient method of farming has thus been preserved through the ages. This relic of the past is interesting from the point of view of quality in food as well as from its historical value.

Rome - The Sword And The Ploughshare

Some other systems of agriculture of the past have come down to us in the form of written records which have furnished ample material for constructive research.

In the case of Rome in particular a fairly complete account of the position of agriculture, from the period of the monarchy to the fall of the Roman Empire, is available; the facts can be conveniently followed in the writings of Mommsen, Heitland, and other scholars. In the case of Rome the

Servian Reform (Servius Tullius, 578-534 B.C.) shows very clearly not only that the agricultural class originally preponderated in the State but also that an effort was made to maintain the collective body of freeholders as the pith and marrow of the community. The conception that the constitution itself rested on the freehold system permeated the whole policy of Roman war and conquest. The aim of war was to increase the number of its freehold members.

'The vanquished community was either compelled to merge entirely into the yeomanry of Rome, or, if not reduced to this extremity, it was required, not to pay a war contribution or a fixed tribute, but to cede a portion, usually a third part, of its domain, which was thereupon regularly occupied by Roman farms.

Many nations have gained victories and made conquests as the Romans did; but none has equalled the Roman in thus making the ground he had won his own by the sweat of his brow, and in securing by the ploughshare what had been gained by the lance.

That which is gained by war may be wrested from the grasp by war again, but it is not so with the conquests made by the plough; whilst the Romans lost many battles, they scarcely ever on making peace ceded Roman soil, and for this result they were indebted to the tenacity with which the farmers clung to their fields and homesteads.

The strength of man and of the State lies in their dominion over the soil; the strength of Rome was built on the most extensive and immediate mastery of her citizens over the soil, and on the compact unity of the body which thus acquired so firm a hold.' (Mommsen)

Capitalist System Vs. Sound Agricultural Practices

Decay Sets In As Large Estates Takeover

These splendid ideals did not persist. During the period which elapsed between the union of Italy and the subjugation of Carthage, a gradual decay of the farmers set in; the small-holdings ceased to yield any substantial clear return; the cultivators one by one faced ruin; the moral tone and frugal habits of the earlier ages of the Republic were lost; the land of the Italian farmers became merged into the larger estates.

The landlord capitalist became the centre of the subject. He not only produced at a cheaper rate than the farmer because he had more land, but he began to use slaves. The same space which in the olden time, when small-holdings prevailed, had supported from a hundred to a hundred and fifty families was now occupied by one family of free persons and about fifty, for the most part unmarried, slaves. 'If this was the remedy by which the decaying national economy was to be restored to vigour, it bore, unhappily, an aspect of extreme resemblance to disease' (Mommsen).

The main causes of this decline appear to have been fourfold: the constant drain on the manhood of the country-side by the legions, which culminated in the two long wars with Carthage; the operations of the Roman capitalist landlords which 'contributed quite as much as Hamilcar and Hannibal to the decline in the vigour and the number of the Italian people' (Mommsen); failure to work out a balanced agriculture between crops and live stock and to maintain the fertility of the soil; the employment of slaves instead of free labourers.

During this period the wholesale commerce of Latium passed into the hands of the large landed proprietors who at the same time were the speculators and capitalists. The natural consequence was the destruction of the middle classes, particularly of the small-holders, and the development of landed and moneyed lords on the one hand and of an agricultural proletariat on the other.

The power of capital was greatly enhanced by the growth of the class of tax-farmers and contractors to whom the State farmed out its indirect revenues for a fixed sum. Subsequent political and social conflicts did not give real relief to the agricultural community.

Colonies founded to secure Roman sovereignty over Italy provided farms for the agricultural proletariat, but the root causes of the decline in agriculture were not removed in spite of the efforts of Cato and other reformers.

A capitalist system of which the apparent interests were fundamentally opposed to a sound agriculture remained supreme. The last half of the second century saw degradation and more and more decadence.

Then came Tiberius Gracchus and the Agrarian Law with the appointment of an official commission to counteract the diminution of the farmer class by the comprehensive establishment of new small-holdings from the whole Italian landed property at the disposal of the State: eighty thousand new Italian farmers were provided with land.

These efforts to restore agriculture to its rightful place in the State were accompanied by many improvements in Roman agriculture which, unfortunately, were most suitable for large estates.

Land no longer able to produce corn became pasture; cattle now roamed over large ranches; the vine and the olive were cultivated with commercial success. These systems of agriculture, however, had to be carried on with slave labour, the supply of which had to be maintained by constant importation.

Such extensive methods of farming naturally failed to supply sufficient food for the population of Italy. Other countries were called upon to furnish essential foodstuffs; province after province was conquered to feed the growing proletariat with corn. These areas in turn slowly yielded to the same decline which had taken place in Italy.

Finally the wealthy classes abandoned the depopulated remnants of the mother country and built themselves a new capital at Constantinople. The situation had to be saved by a migration to fresh lands. In their new capital the Romans relied on the unexhausted fertility of Egypt as well as on that of Asia Minor and the Balkan and Danubian provinces.

Judged by the ordinary standards of achievement the agricultural history of the Roman Empire ended in failure due to inability to realize the fundamental principle that the maintenance of soil fertility coupled with the legitimate claims of the agricultural population should never have been allowed to come in conflict with the operations of the capitalist. The most important possession of a country is its population. If this is maintained in health and vigour everything else will follow; if this is allowed to decline nothing, not even great riches, can save the country from eventual ruin. It follows, therefore, that the strongest possible support of capital must always be a prosperous and contented country-side. *A working compromise between agriculture and finance should therefore have been evolved. Failure to achieve this naturally ended in the ruin of both.*

(From An Agricultural Testament)

27

Peak Grain

Forget Oil, Worry About Food

World is witnessing major price hikes in food, as 'peak grains' join the lineup of lifestyle-changing events along with peak oil and peak water. All societies more complex than hunter-gatherers depend on agriculture to survive. This fundamental fact is easily ignored in shopping centers of giant urban metropolises, but the advent of electronic technology, petroleum combustion and globalized economies does not reduce the need for someone, somewhere to grow the food that all of us eat.

Now that Peak Oil and climate change are no longer distant concerns but are the reality of daily events, the impact of these twin crises upon the global food supply is an urgent situation without precedent in history. Peak Oil threatens to remove key energy inputs for industrial agriculture and climate

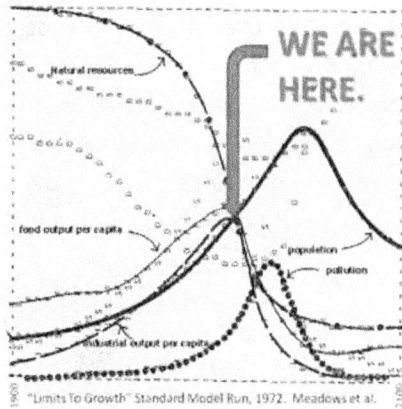

"Limits To Growth" Standard Model Run, 1972. Meadows et al.

change is starting to destabilize growing conditions that make large scale food production possible. This was experienced in 1973 when abysmally low inventories of wheat and an Arab-Israeli war sparked off an oil embargo, runaway global inflation, and upheavals that have scarred societies till today.

The world's is ever-decreasing number of farmers do not produce enough staple grains to feed the world. That is a crisis of quiet desperation over the past decade for the 15,000 people who die each day from hunger-related causes. It is also about to cause a problem for people who assumed that the sheer unavailability of food basics, usually seen as a problem of dire poverty, would never cause a problem for them. People in rich nations are also now waking up to possibilities of food shortages.

Reference

Mark Robinowitz, Peak Grain: Feeding Nine Billion After Peak Oil and Climate Change, Oil Empire, December 2006

Could we really run out of food?", Jon Markman, March 6, 2008

28

Agricutural Practices of The East

Permanent And Have Passed The Supreme Test of Time

By Sir Albert Howard, 1940

In the agriculture of Asia we find ourselves confronted with a system of peasant farming which in essentials soon became stabilized. What is happening to-day in the small fields of India and China took-place many centuries ago. There is here no need to study historical records or to pay a visit to the remains of the megalithic farming of the Andes.

The agricultural practices of the Orient have passed the supreme test—they are almost as permanent as those of the primeval forest, of the prairie or of the ocean. The small holdings of China, for example, are still maintaining a steady output and there is no loss of fertility after forty centuries of management.

What are the chief characteristics of this Eastern farming? The holdings are minute. Taking India as an example, the relation between man power and cultivated area is referred to in the Census Report of 1931 as follows: 'For every agriculturalist there is 2.9 acres of cropped land of which 0.65 of an acre is irrigated. The corresponding figures of 1921 are 2.7 and 0.61.'

These figures illustrate how intense is the struggle for existence in this portion of the tropics. These small-holdings are often cultivated by extensive methods (those suitable for large areas) which utilize neither the full energies of man or beast nor the potential fertility of the soil.

If we turn to the Far East, to China and Japan, a similar system of small-holdings is accompanied by an even more intense pressure of population both human and bovine.

In the introduction to Farmers of Forty Centuries, King states that the three main islands of Japan had in 1907 a population of 46,977,000, maintained on 20,000 square miles of cultivated fields. This is at the rate of 2,349 to the square mile or more than three people to each acre.

In addition, Japan fed on each square mile of cultivation a very large animal population—69 horses and 56 cattle, nearly all employed in labour; 825 poultry; 13 swine, goats, and sheep.

Although no accurate statistics are available in China, the examples quoted by King reveal a condition of affairs not unlike that in Japan. In the Shantung Province a farmer with a family of twelve kept one donkey, one cow, and two pigs on 2.5 acres of cultivated land—a density of population at the rate of 3,072 people, 256 donkeys, 256 cattle, and 512 pigs per square mile.

The average of seven Chinese holdings visited gave a maintenance capacity of 1,783 people, 212 cattle or donkeys, and 399 pigs—nearly 2,000 consumers and 400 rough food transformers per square mile of farmed land. In comparison with these remarkable figures, the corresponding statistics for 1900 in the case of the United States per square mile were: population 61, horses and mules 30.

Two Hungers—The Stomach And The Machine

Food and forage crops are predominant. *The primary function of Eastern agriculture is to supply the cultivators and their cattle with food.* This automatically follows because of the pressure of the population on the land: *the main hunger the soil has to appease is that of the stomach. A subsidiary hunger is that of the machine which needs raw materials for manufacture.*

This extra hunger is new but has developed considerably since the opening of the Suez Canal in 1869 (by which the small fields of the cultivator have been brought into effective contact with the markets of the West) and the establishment of local industries like cotton and jute. To both these hungers soil fertility has to respond. We know from long experience that the fields of India can respond to the hunger of the stomach.

Whether they can fulfil the added demands of the machine remains to be seen. The Suez Canal has only been in operation for seventy years. The first cotton mill in India was opened in 1818 at Fort Gloster, near Calcutta. The jute industry of Bengal has grown up within a century. Jute was first exported in 1838. The first jute mill on the Hoogly began operations in 1855.

These local industries as well as the export trade in raw products for the use of the factories of the West are an extra drain on soil fertility. Their future wellbeing and indeed their very existence is only possible provided adequate steps are taken to maintain this fertility.

There is obviously no point in establishing cotton and jute mills in India, in founding trading agencies like those of Calcutta and in building ships for the conveyance of raw products unless such enterprises are stable and permanent. It would be folly and an obvious waste of capital to pursue such activities if they are founded only on the existing store of soil fertility.

All concerned in the hunger of the machine— government, financiers, manufacturers, and distributors—must see to it that the fields of India are equal to the new burden which has been thrust upon her during the last fifty years or so. The demands of commerce and industry on the one hand and the fertility of the soil on the other must be maintained in correct relation the one to the other.

The response of India to the two hungers—the stomach and the machine—will be evident from a study of Table 1, in which the area in acres under food and fodder crops is compared with that under money crops. The chief food crops in order of importance are rice, pulses, millets, wheat, and fodder crops. The money crops are more varied; cotton and oil seeds are the most important, followed by jute and other fibres, tobacco, tea, coffee, and opium. It will be seen that food and fodder crops comprise 86 percent of the total area under crops and that money crops, as far as extent is concerned, are less important, and constitute only one-seventh of the total cultivated area.

One interesting change in the production of Indian food crops has taken place during the last twenty-five years. The output of sugar used to be insufficient for the towns, and large quantities were imported from Java, Mauritius, and the continent of Europe. Today, thanks to the work at Shahjahanpur in the United Provinces, the new varieties of cane bred at Coimbatore and the protection now enjoyed by the sugar industry, India is almost self-supporting as far as sugar is concerned. The pre-war average amount of sugar imported was 634,000 tons; in 1937-8 the total had fallen to 14,000 tons.

TABLE I

Agricultural Statistics of British India, 1935-36 Area, in acres, under food and fodder crops

Rice	79,888,000
Millets	38,144,000
Wheat	25,150,000
Gram	14,897,000
Pulses and other food grains	29,792,000

Fodder crops	10,791,000
Condiments, spices, fruits, vegetables, and miscellaneous food crops	8,308,000
Barley	6,178,000
Maize	6,211,000
Sugar	4,038,000
Total, food and fodder crops	223,397,000
Area, in acres, under money crops	
Cotton	15,761,000
Oil seeds, chiefly ground-nuts, sesamum, rape, mustard, and linseed	15,662,000
Jute and other fibres	2,706,000
Dyes, tanning materials, drugs, narcotics, and miscellaneous money crops	1,458,000
Tobacco	1,230,000
Tea	787,000
Coffee	97,000
Indigo	40,000
Opium	10,000
Total, money crops	37,751,000

Following In Nature's Footsteps

Mixed crops are the rule. In this respect the cultivators of the Orient have followed Nature's method as seen in the primeval forest. Mixed cropping is perhaps most universal when the cereal crop is the main constituent. Crops like millets, wheat, barley, and maize are mixed with an appropriate subsidiary pulse, sometimes a species that ripens much later than the cereal.

The pigeon pea (Cajanus indicus Spreng.), perhaps the most important leguminous crop of the Gangetic alluvium, is grown either with millets or with maize. The mixing of cereals and pulses appears to help both crops. When the two grow together the character of the growth improves.

Do the roots of these crops excrete materials useful to each other? Is the mycorrhizal association found in the roots of these tropical legumes and cereals the agent involved in this excretion? Science at the moment is unable to answer these questions: it is only now beginning to investigate them.

Here we have another instance where the peasants of the East have anticipated and acted upon the solution of one of the problems which Western science is only just beginning to recognize. Whatever may be the reason why crops thrive best when associated in suitable combinations, the fact remains that mixtures generally give better results than monoculture.

This is seen in Great Britain in the growth of dredge corn, in mixed crops of wheat and beans, vetches and rye, clover and rye-grass, and in intensive vegetable growing under glass. The produce raised under Dutch lights has noticeably increased since the mixed cropping of the Chinese vegetable growers of Australia has been copied. Mr. F. A. Secrett was, I believe, the first to introduce this system on a large scale into Great Britain. He

So *that's* what those 40 thieves have been stealing and hoarding.

informed me that he saw it for the first time at Melbourne.

A balance between live stock and crops is always maintained. Although crops are generally more important than animals in Eastern agriculture, we seldom or never find crops without animals. This is because oxen are required for cultivation and buffaloes for milk. Nevertheless, the waste products of the animal, as is often the case in other parts of the world, are not always fully utilized for the land.

The Chinese have for ages past recognized the importance of the urine of animals and the great value of animal wastes in the preparation of composts. In India far less attention is paid to these wastes and a large portion of the cattle dung available is burnt for fuel.

Although half a million examples of the connection between a fertile soil and a healthy plant exist in India alone, and these natural experiments have been in operation for centuries before experiment stations like Rothamsted were ever thought of, modern agricultural science takes no notice of the results and resolutely refuses to accept them as evidence, largely because they lack the support furnished by the higher mathematics.

Leguminous plants are common. Although it was not till 1888, after a protracted controversy lasting thirty years, that Western science finally accepted as proved the important part played by pulse crops in enriching the soil, centuries of experience had taught the peasants of the East the same lesson.

The leguminous crop in the rotation is everywhere one of their old fixed practices. In some areas, such as the Indo-Gangetic plain, one of these pulses—the pigeon pea—is also made use of as a subsoil cultivator. The deep spreading root system is used to promote the aeration of the closely packed silt soils, which so closely resemble those of the Holland Division of Lincolnshire in Great Britain.

Cultivation is generally superficial and is carried out by wooden ploughs furnished with an iron point. Soil-inverting ploughs, as used in the West for the destruction of weeds, have never been designed by Eastern peoples.

The reasons for this appear to be two: (1) soil inversion for the destruction of weeds is not necessary in a hot climate where the same work is done by the sun for nothing; (2) the preservation of the level of the fields is essential for surface drainage, for preventing local waterlogging, and for irrigation.

Another reason for this surface cultivation has recently been pointed out. The store of nitrogen in the soil in the form of organic matter has to be carefully conserved: it is part of the cultivator's working capital. Too much cultivation and deep ploughing would oxidize this reserve and the balance of soil fertility would soon be destroyed.

Rice is grown whenever possible. By far the most important crop in the East is rice. In India, as has already been pointed out, the production of rice exceeds that of any two food crops put together,

Whenever the soil and water supply permit, rice is invariably grown. A study of this crop is illuminating. At first sight rice appears to contradict one of the great principles of the agricultural science of the West, namely, the dependence of cereals on nitrogenous manures.

Large crops of rice are produced in many parts of India on the same land year after year without the addition of any manure whatever. The rice fields of the country export paddy in large quantities to the centres of population or abroad, but there is no corresponding import of combined nitrogen. Where does the rice crop obtain its nitrogen? One source in all probability is fixation from the atmosphere in the submerged algal film on the surface of the mud. Another is the rice nursery itself, where the seedlings are raised on land heavily manured with cattle dung.

Large quantities of nitrogen and other nutrients are stored in the seedling itself; this at transplanting time contains a veritable arsenal of reserves of all kinds which carry the plant successfully through this process and probably also furnish some of the nitrogen needed during subsequent growth. The manuring of the rice seedling illustrates a very general principle in agriculture, namely, the importance of starting a crop in a really fertile soil and so arranging matters that the plant can absorb a great deal of what it needs as early as possible in its development.

There is an adequate supply of labour. Labour is everywhere abundant, as would naturally follow from the great density of the rural population. Indeed, in India it is so great that if the leisure

time of the cultivators and their cattle for a single year could be calculated as money at the local rates a perfectly colossal figure would be obtained. This leisure, however, is not altogether wasted. It enables the cultivators and their oxen to recover from the periods of intensive work which precede the sowing of the crops and which are needed at harvest time. At these periods time is everything: everybody works from sunrise to sunset. The preparation of the land and the sowing of the crops need the greatest care and skill; the work must be completed in a very short time so that a large labour force is essential.

Taking Burma as an example of an area exporting rice beyond seas, during the twenty years ending 1924, about 25,000,000 tons of paddy have been exported from a tract roughly 10,000,000 acres in area. As unhusked rice contains about 1.2 percent of nitrogen the amount of this element, shipped overseas during twenty years or destroyed in the burning of the husk, is in the neighbourhood of 300,000 tons.

As this constant drain of nitrogen is not made up for by the import of manure, we should expect to find a gradual loss of fertility. Nevertheless, this does not take place either in Burma or in Bengal, where rice has been grown on the same land year after year for centuries. Clearly the soil must obtain fresh supplies of nitrogen from somewhere, otherwise the crop would cease to grow. The only likely source is fixation from the atmosphere, probably in the submerged algal film on the surface of the mud. This is one of the problems of tropical agriculture which is now being investigated.

It will be observed that in this peasant agriculture the great pressure of population on the soil results in poverty, most marked where, as in India, extensive methods are used on small-holdings which really need intensive farming. It is amazing that in spite of this unfavourable factor soil fertility should have been preserved for centuries: *this is because natural means have been used and not artificial manures. The crops are able to withstand the inroads of insects and fungi* without a thin film of protective poison.

Bibliography

Agricultural Statistics Of India, I, Delhi, 1938.

Howard, A., And Howard, G. L. C. The Development Of Indian Agriculture, Oxford University Press, 1929.

King, F. H. Farmers Of Forty Centuries Or Permanent Agriculture In China, Korea, And Japan, London, 1926.

We know when India was more primitive, there were thousands of cows owned by the agriculturists and they used to enjoy life by the agricultural products and sufficient quantity of clarified butter, milk and curd. Even some hundreds of years before during the reign of Nawab Swaesta Khan, rice was selling in India at the rate of nine mounds (40kg x9) a rupee and today ever since the beginning of scientific knowledge in India, rice is selling now at the rate of nine chatak (60gms x9) a rupee. In the former days, the Indian kings and rich men used to perform yajnas by burning tons and tons of pure clarified butter made out of cow's milk and at the present moment there is not a drop of pure clarified butter made out of cow's milk even for daily use. That is the law of material nature. Leaving aside the stories of Nawab Sawesta Khan's history we can say from our personal experience that my father say 40 years before at most used to stock at our house (in Calcutta) always a cart load of rice, 15 mounds (40kg x15), ten seers (1kg x10) of pure ghee, a bag of potato and a cart load of soft coke always ready for use. Our family was not a rich family and my father's income was within Rs. 250/- per month. And it was within his easy reach to stock household provisions in the above manner. But at the present moment at no house in the cities and towns generally there is stock of more than 15 seers (1kg x15) of rice. Formerly they used to enquire rates of commodities in the terms of mounds (40kg) and now they ask for it in terms of seers (1kg) or chattacks (60gms) although we are able to keep more glittering cars than cows at the present moment.

— Srila Prabhupada (Back To Godhead magazine, Nov. 1956)

29

Farmers' Suicides

Indications of A Failing Agriculture In India

According to Gandhi's vision of Gram-swaraj, villages and farmers were to be the main focus of any development plan in India. As years passed, agriculture as an industry lost its importance to policy makers. Over a time, this caused severe distress among the farmers leading to recent dramatic rise in the number of suicides among farmer community. Every day in national newspaper invariably there is some news related to farmers' suicides.

India, consisting of 16% of world's population, sustains only on 2.4% of land resource. Agriculture sector is the only livelihood to the two-third of its population which gives employment to the 57% of work force and is a raw material source to large number of industries.

In 1990s, India woke-up to a spate of suicide among farmers community. The first state to report suicides was Maharashtra.

Since long time, Indian farmers have been facing a number of socioeconomic problems, such as harassment by moneylenders,

inability to repay debts following crop losses, lack of health care etc. The problem is compounded by lack of support from banks especially in the face of inclement weather and market fluctuations. Economic plight of farmers might be illustrated with the fact that a farmer having as much as 15 acres of land and hence considered a well off farmer in Vidarbha, with an average income of Rs 2700 per acre per annum, had an income just little more than what he would have earned the legal minimum wage for all 365 days of the year.

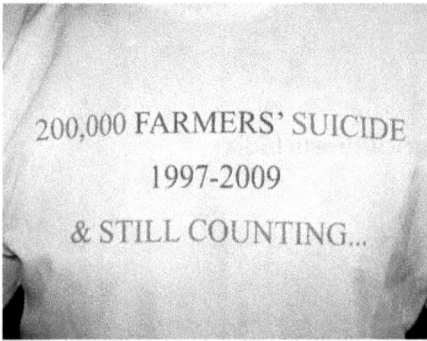

> But the same India was producing so much grains, even during British time, that many thousands and thousand tons of rice were being exported from India to other countries. You see? That I have seen. I have seen. My maternal uncle was very rich man by simply exporting rice to the foreign countries. Yes. Spices... And old history you will find that India, they had got their own ships for exporting spices to Greece and other countries of Europe. The history is there. And they were supplying muslin cloth, even just before the British period, Muslim period. So India's export, export, I mean to say, status was far greater than other countries. And these spices and other export attracted persons from Europe, that Vasco de Gama, and the Columbus also wanted to go, but he fortunately came to America. You see? All these Europeans and the Britishers went and established their supremacy. So India was so rich. But now how that India has become so poor? The same land is there. Why? Because they have lost that old culture, God consciousness. You see? But in the same India... You just read the history, five thousand years before, how much profusely the nature was supplying.
> ~ Srila Prabhupada (Bhagavad-gita 2.48-49 -- New York, April 1, 1966)

In a country of 70 million farmers, 10 in every 100,000 are committing suicide. This is higher than the total national suicide rate. Over 16,600 farmer committed suicide in 2007 which work out to 2 suicides every hour. Farmer suicides in the country for the period 1997-2007 now total 182,936.

30

The Agricultural Methods Of The West

Impermanent And Utterly Destructive

By Sir Albert Howard, 1940

If we take a wide survey of the contribution which is being made by the fields of the West, we find that they are engaged in trying to satisfy no less than three hungers: (1) the local hunger of the rural population, including the live stock; (2) the hunger of the growing urban areas, the population of which is unproductive from the point of view of soil fertility; and (3) the hunger of the machine avid for a constant stream of the raw materials required for manufacture.

The urban population during the last century has grown out of all knowledge; the needs of the machine increase as it becomes more and more efficient; falling profits are met by increasing the output of manufactured articles. All this adds to the burden on the land and to the calls on its fertility.

It will not be without interest to analyze critically the agriculture of the West and see how it is fitting itself for its growing task.

> *"Western civilization is a loaded gun pointed at the head of this planet."*
> ~*Terence McKenna*

This can be done by examining its main characteristics. These are as follows: The holding tends to increase in size. There is a great variation in the size of the agricultural holdings of the West from the small family units of France and Switzerland to the immense collective farms of Russia and the spacious ranches of the United States and Argentina.

Side by side with this growth in the size of the farm is the diminution of the number of men per square mile. In Canada, for example, the number of workers per 1,000 acres of cropped land fell from 26 in 1911 to 16 in 1926. Since these data were published the size of the working population has shrunk still further. This state of things has arisen from the scarcity and dearness of labour which has naturally led to the study of labour-saving devices.

Monoculture is the rule. Almost everywhere crops are grown in pure culture. Except in temporary leys, mixed crops are rare. On the rich prairie lands of North America even rotations are unknown: *crops of wheat follow one another and no attempt is made to convert the straw into humus by means of the urine and dung of cattle.* The straw is a tiresome encumbrance and is burnt off annually.

The machine is rapidly replacing the animal. Increasing mechanization is one of the main features of Western agriculture.

Whenever a machine can be invented which saves human or animal labour its spread is rapid. Engines and motors of various kinds are the rule everywhere. The electrification of agriculture is beginning. The inevitable march of the combine harvester in all the wheat producing areas of the world is one of the latest examples of the mechanization of the agriculture of the West.

Cultivation tends to be quicker and deeper. There is a growing feeling that the more and the deeper the soil is stirred the better will be the crop. The invention of the gyrotiller, a heavy and expensive soil churn, is one of the answers to this demand. The slaves of the Roman Empire have been replaced by mechanical slaves.

Machines Do Not Produce Urine And Dung

The replacement of the horse and the ox by the internal combustion engine and the electric motor is, however, attended by one great disadvantage. *These machines do not produce urine and dung and so contribute nothing to the maintenance of soil fertility*. In this sense the slaves of Western agriculture are less efficient than those of ancient Rome.

Artificial manures are widely used. The feature of the manuring of the West is the use of artificial manures. The factories engaged during the Great War in the fixation of atmospheric nitrogen for the manufacture of explosives had to find other markets, the use of nitrogenous fertilizers in agriculture increased, until today the majority of farmers and market gardeners base their manurial programme on the cheapest forms of nitrogen (N), phosphorus (P), and potassium (K) on the market. What may be conveniently described as the NPK mentality dominates farming alike in the experimental stations and the country-side. Vested interests, entrenched in time of national emergency, have gained a stranglehold.

Without Animals, All Agricultural Technologies Are Bound To Fail

Artificial manures involve less labour and less trouble than farm-yard manure. The tractor is superior to the horse in power and in speed of work: it needs no food and no expensive care during its long hours of rest. These two agencies have made it easier to run a farm. A satisfactory profit and loss account has been obtained. For the moment farming has been made to pay. But there is another side to this picture. *These chemicals and these machines can do nothing to keep the soil in good heart.* By their use the processes of growth can never be balanced by the processes of decay. All that they can accomplish is the transfer of the soil's capital to current account.

That this is so will be much clearer when the attempts now being made to farm without any animals at all march to their inevitable failure.

Diseases are on the increase. With the spread of artificials and the exhaustion of the original supplies of humus, carried by every fertile

Here it is said that avidya-kama-karmabhih. By ignorance, they are thinking by opening factories they will be happy. That is avidya. He does not know that this is ignorance. Why you should open factory? That is... This is called ugra-karma. There is no need of opening factory. You have got land. Here are so many lands. You produce your food grains. Annad bhavanti bhutani [Bg. 3.14]. You eat sumptuously food grain, milk, and that will be available without any factory. The factory cannot produce milk or food grain. The present scarcity of foodstuff means everybody is engaged in the city, producing bolts and nuts. Who is producing food grain? This is the solution of economic problem. Annad bhavanti bhutani. Therefore we are trying to engage our men to produce their own food. Be self-sufficient so that these rascals may see that how one can live very peacefully, eating the food grains and milk, and chant Hare Krsna.

~ Srila Prabhupada (Srimad-Bhagavatam 1.8.35 -- Mayapur, October 15, 1974)

soil, there has been a corresponding increase in the diseases of crops and of the animals which feed on them. If the spread of foot-and-mouth disease in Europe and its comparative insignificance among well fed animals in the East are compared, or if the comparison is made between certain areas in Europe, the conclusion is inevitable that there must be an intimate connection between faulty methods of agriculture and animal disease.

In crops like potatoes and fruit, the use of the poison spray has closely followed the reduction in the supplies of farm-yard manure and the diminution of fertility.

Food preservation processes are also on the increase. A feature of the agriculture of the West is the development of food preservation

Modern Farming

HE SCARES OFF THE CROWS.
I SCARE OFF
MONSANTO.

processes by which the journey of products like meat, milk, vegetables, and fruit between the soil and the stomach is prolonged. This is done by freezing, by the use of carbon dioxide, by drying, and by canning. Although food is preserved for a time in this way, what is the effect of these processes on the health of the community during a period of, say, twenty-five years? Is it possible to preserve the first freshness of food? If so then science will have made a very real contribution.

Science has been called in to help production. Another of the features of the agriculture of the West is the development of agricultural science. Efforts have been made to enlist the help of a number of separate sciences in studying the problems of agriculture and in increasing the production of the soil. This has entailed the foundation of numerous experiment stations which every year pour out a large volume of advice in the shape of printed matter.

Mother Earth Deprived Of Her Manurial Rights, Is In Revolt

*These mushroom ideas of agriculture are failing; mother earth deprived of her **manurial rights** is in revolt; the land is going on strike; the fertility of the soil is declining.* An examination of the areas which feed the population and the machines of a country like Great Britain leaves no doubt that the soil is no longer able to stand the strain. Soil fertility is rapidly diminishing, particularly in the United States, Canada, Africa, Australia, and New Zealand. In Great Britain itself real farming has already been given up except on the best lands.

The loss of fertility all over the world is indicated by the growing menace of soil erosion. The seriousness of the situation is proved by the attention now being paid to this matter in the press and by the various Administrations. In the United States, for example, the whole resources of government are being mobilized to save what is left of the good earth.

The agricultural record has been briefly reviewed from the standpoint of soil fertility. The main characteristics of the various methods of agriculture have been summarized. The most significant of these are the operations of Nature as seen in the forest. There the fullest use is made of sunlight and rainfall in raising heavy crops of produce and at the same time not only maintaining fertility but actually building up large reserves of humus.

The peasants of China, who pay great attention to the return of all wastes to the land, come nearest to the ideal set by Nature. They have maintained a large population on the land without any falling off in fertility.

The agriculture of ancient Rome failed because it was unable to maintain the soil in a fertile condition. The farmers of the West are repeating the mistakes made by Imperial Rome. The soils of the Roman Empire, however, were only called upon to assuage the hunger of a relatively small population. The demands of the machine were then almost non-existent. In the West there are relatively more stomachs to fill while the growing hunger of the machine is an additional burden on the soil. The Roman Empire lasted for eleven centuries.

How long will the supremacy of the West endure? The answer depends on the wisdom and courage of the population in dealing with the things that matter. Can mankind regulate its affairs so that its chief possession—the fertility of the soil—is preserved? On the answer to this question the future of civilization depends.

Bibliography

Lymington, Viscount. Famine In England, London, 1938.

Mommsen, Theodor. The History Of Rome, Transl. Dickson, London, 1894.

Wrench, G. T. The Wheel Of Health, London, 1938.

31

Diminishing Nutrition In Foods

The biggest problem with foods of the modern civilization is their so called refinement or purification. We have to eat them as the nature intended us to do. Experiments revealed that animals fed on a diet composed of purified proteins, purified starches, purified fats and inorganic salts, although they may live on these for a time, do not grow and in a short time develop various pathological conditions as a result of such "diet." If whey, or fruit juice, or vegetables are then added to the diet, the symptoms improve and the animals thrive better.

People now a days regularly consume breakfasts such as this one: a denatured cereal with white sugar and pasteurized cream, toast (white), pasteurized milk and, perhaps, bacon and eggs. Every article in this breakfast is denatured and altered chemically to a great extent. It is a predominantly acid forming breakfast and yet, the vitamin faddist will tell us only that it is lacking vitamin C or D. Our vitamin knowledge, where

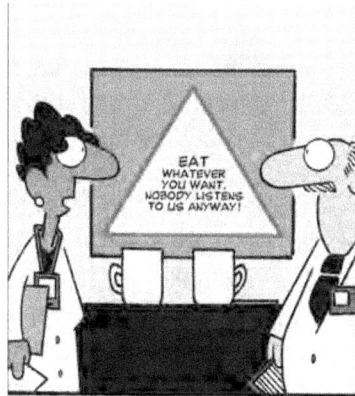

"They revised the Food Pyramid again."

111

it is permitted to obscure all else, as is usually the case, certainly blinds so-called dietitians to some of the most important facts and principles of food science.

Except for the fresh fruits and vegetables we eat, practically everything we have on our table has had something done to it. Our milk is pasteurized, condensed, evaporated, boiled; Our sugar is the crystallized, refined and bleached sap of cane that has had all the minerals and vitamins removed from it. Our cereals are cracked, rolled, hammered, frittered, curled, flaked, ironed, roasted, twice roasted, boiled, and in other ways rendered useless. Wheat is milled, its minerals and vitamins removed, the flour is bleached and chemicalized. Its most important food elements are removed in the milling process. Our dried fruits are heated in drying, bleached with sulphur dioxide, stored for long

Heaven is under our feet as well as over our heads
Henry David Thoreau

periods of time and, finally, stewed and mixed with white sugar before being eaten.

The refining, preserving and cooking processes to which our foods are subjected destroy extraordinarily delicate and tender vital food factors. The refining and cooking processes rob foods of so much of their values that we add salt, sugar, spices, pepper and various other condiments and seasonings to them to make them palatable. Without the additions of such things they are dull, flat, insipid. Not so natural foods. Nature has placed delicate flavors and aromas in her foods that appeal to the senses of taste and smell.

A nation whose diet is made up almost wholly of such 'foodless' foods cannot possibly be well nourished. Why go to great lengths and much trouble to build up our soils and then take everything out of the foods that the 'improved' soils have put into them?

Over eighty years ago, Dr. Magendie, of Paris, starved one full pen of dogs to death by feeding them a diet of white flour and water, while another pen thrived on whole wheat flour and water. He fed another pen of dogs all the beef tea they could consume, and gave the dogs of another pen only water. The beef tea fed dogs all starved to death. The water fed dogs had lost considerable weight and would have starved also if the experiment had been continued; however, they were alive after those fed on beef tea were all dead. They were fed and all recovered.

Dogs fed on oil, gum or sugar died in four to five weeks. Dogs fed on fine (white) flour bread lived but fifty days. A goose fed on sugar in twenty-one days; two fed on starch died in twenty-four and twenty-seven days.

"Pulling open the bag and chewing all the chips burns more calories than leaving the bag on the shelf!"

Reference

Shelton, Herbert M. The Hygienic System, Vol. II, Orthotrophy.

Just like I have several times told you that Krsna says, annad bhavanti bhutani [Bg. 3.14]. Bhavanti means you flourish, you become healthy. Your mind becomes sound. Your brain becomes sound. If you eat properly, naturally... Just like the stomach must be satisfied. If the stomach is satisfied, you get the energy immediately. Different energy is produced, different secretion is produced, and one secretion is sent to the heart, one secretion... That is medical science. And then it is turned into blood, and there are different veins, it is distributed all over the... This big machine is going on like a big factory; simply you have to give the raw materials to the factory, and things will come out.

~ Srila Prabhupada (Srimad-Bhagavatam 1.8.36 -- Mayapur, October 16, 1974)

32

Soil Depletion

Plant, Animal And Human Health Deterioration

Soil and organic matter in the soil may be considered our most important national resource. Plant and animal health and subsequently human health depends on healthy soil. Unfortunately our current farm practices have enormously reduced the supply originally present in the soil and we must expect a permanently lower level of agricultural efficiency if we do not take corrective steps urgently. An adequate supply of organic matter in the soil is vital to the survival of life on the planet.

One of the factors responsible for the global health crisis today is soil deterioration. In the Museum of Natural History (New York), is an exhibit showing the effects of soil deficiency on plant life.

These plants, all of the same kind, were reared in soils lacking some element. The exhibit has to be seen to be fully appreciated. The plants range in size from about three inches to about eighteen inches in height. Their color ranges from pale yellow to dark green. The leaves of some are broad, of others narrow. Some of the leaves are kinky. All of the plants except one is defective both in size, color and features and all except that one were raised in soil lacking some food element. For example, one was raised in a soil lacking iron, (the plant has "anemia"), another in a soil lacking potassium, another in a soil lacking nitrogen, etc.

Deficient soil means deficient food that grows on it. Humans and animals who consume such food also naturally become nutrient deficient. If essential food elements are lacking in their foods, they, like the plants in the experiments, fail and die. Ride along the highway with an experienced farmer and he will point out fertile soil and poor soil, by the vegetation growing thereon; sickly and stunted children (as well as the obese ones) are the result of poor soil.

Empty Foods, Hollow Lives

We've all heard and read it countless times - "the best way to maintain health is to eat a balanced diet including lots of fruit and vegetables". Of course, this is absolutely correct, so long as those fruits and vegetables are not grown on the mineral-depleted soils that necessitate todays ever-increasing range of chemical 'fertilizers'.

As long ago as in 1920s, the British and US Governments were warned by nutritional experts that the soils on which most crops were grown were so deficient in mineral content that the foods grown on them contained less than 10% of the vitamins and minerals they should normally have. The intention of these reports was to highlight the problem so that remedial action could be taken to remineralise the soils, leading once again to naturally healthy fruits and vegetables.

But in last one century, no remedial action has been taken and the problem has been intensified by modern intensive farming methods. The fruits and vegetables not only have little or no vitamin and mineral content, but they are routinely sprayed with such a broad selection of chemicals that they are actually poisonous.

How Can Plants Grow Without Vitamins And Minerals?

They can! Even when the soil is burnt out, farmers can still grow good looking fruits and vegetables. Most plants require only three nutrients to grow, namely nitrogen, phosphorus and water. In the presence of these nutrients, virtually all plants will grow into what appear to be healthy, nutritious adult specimens.

However, if the minerals found in their natural habitat are not present, such plants and their relevant fruits and vegetables will be nutritionally "empty".

As a result of this, these plants are less able to defend themselves against natural predators and are susceptible to insect attack and damage from viruses / bacteria. In order to control this, insecticides, antifungals, antibiotics, pesticides and dozens of other categories of chemicals have been designed to limit the damage done to plants by their natural enemies.

Unfortunately, many of these chemicals have not been properly tested to assess their effects on either plant or human health, and virtually none have been tested in combination to assess their combined effects. The result is that most fruits, vegetables and other plant-based foods are so contaminated with a huge variety of chemicals, and so deficient in nutrient content that they actually do more harm than good.

> *Many may claim that in the modern age material scientists have helped increase agricultural yield. But we fearlessly proclaim that it is precisely such atheistic views that have brought the world to the present acute food crisis. If we are not careful, the day will soon come when fruits will be reduced to just skin and seed, cows' udders will dry up, and paddy fields will grow only grass. The scriptures predict that these things will come to pass in the Kali-yuga.*
>
> *~Srila Prabhupada, Renunciation Through Wisdom 2.10*

33

Deterioration of Diet

Eating Anything and Everything

The standard of eating all over the world is rapidly deteriorating. Global population is eating lessser quality foods then they did years back. The deterioration in the composition of the diet can be seen by looking in more detail at the constituent food groups that make up the diet. We can take the example of let's say, Nigeria.

Figure shows the relative percentages of the different food groups that make up the total annual food utilized in the country, in 1963, and then in 1990.

The largest component is starchy roots, about 56% of the diet in 1963. In 1990, this has gone up to almost 67% of the diet. Mostly, this is cassava, which, along with a variety

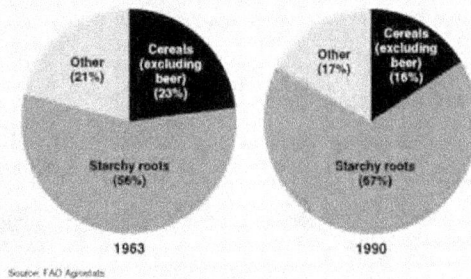

FIGURE 24
Nigeria food production, 1963 and 1990
percent of total annual food utilized

Source: FAO Agrostats

of companion foods, is part of West African cuisines. However, the increased use of cassava from 1963 to 1990 reflects not a dietary preference, but rather a forced reliance on the root vegetable as a heavy-bearing crop, on which people can subsist, i.e., it's filling, but not nutritious.

What is shown as the "other" segment on the Nigeria food charts, is the total of all 12 other food types. In 1990, this included 5.4% vegetables; 3.5% fruits; 2% peas and beans; 1.6% sugar crops; 1% meats, and even lesser amounts of the remaining food groups.

Reference

December 8, 1995 issue of Executive Intelligence Review.

The whole world is coming to like that. And it is said in the sastra, gradually this condition of human civilization will deteriorate to such extent that no more rice will be available, no more wheat will be available, no more sugar will be available. Everything will be... No more milk will be available. Finished. Simply you have to eat the seeds of the... There is not fruit, only seed. Just like in the mango, there is one seed and pulp. The pulp will not be available, only seed will be available. These are already foretold. No fruits will be available, no grains will be available, no milk will be available.

~ Srila Prabhupada (Srimad-Bhagavatam 5.5.3 -- Stockholm, September 9, 1973)

34

Death Of Soil

A Result Of The Policy Failure

By Sir Albert Howard, 1940

Perhaps the most widespread and the most important disease of the soil at the present time is soil erosion, a phase of infertility to which great attention is now being paid. Soil erosion in the very mild form of denudation has been in operation since the beginning of time. It is one of the normal operations of Nature going on everywhere. The minute soil particles which result from the decay of rocks find their way sooner or later to the ocean, but many may linger on the way, often for centuries, in the form of one of the constituents of fertile fields.

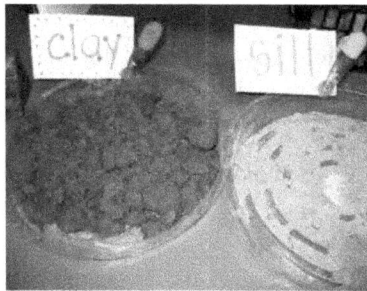

This phenomenon can be observed in any river valley. The fringes of the catchment area are frequently uncultivated hills through the thin soils of which the underlying rocks protrude. These are constantly weathered and in the process yield a continuous supply of minute fragments in all stages of decomposition.

The slow rotting of exposed rock surfaces is only one of the forms of decay. The covering of soil is no protection to the underlying strata but rather the reverse, because the soil water, containing carbon dioxide in solution is constantly disintegrating the parent rock, first producing sub-soil and then actual soil. At the same time the remains of plants and animals are converted into humus. The fine soil particles of mineral origin, often mixed with fragments of humus, are then gradually removed by rain, wind, snow, or ice to lower regions. Ultimately the rich valley lands are reached where the accumulations may be many feet in thickness.

One of the main duties of the streams and rivers, which drain the valley, is to transport these soil particles into the sea where fresh land can be laid down. The process looked at as a whole is nothing more than Nature's method of the rotation, not of the crop, but of the soil itself.

When the time comes for the new land to be enclosed and brought into cultivation agriculture is born again. Such operations are well seen in England in Holbeach marsh and similar areas round the Wash. From the time of the Romans to the present day, new areas of fertile soil, which now fetch £100 an acre or even more, have been re-created from the uplands by the Welland, the Nen, and the Ouse. All this fertile land, perhaps the most valuable in England, is the result of two of the most widespread processes in Nature— weathering and denudation.

It is when the tempo of denudation is vastly accelerated by human agencies that a perfectly harmless natural process becomes transformed into a definite disease of the soil. The condition known as soil erosion—a man-made disease—is then established. It is, however, always preceded by infertility: the inefficient, overworked, dying soil is at once removed by the operations of Nature and hustled towards the ocean, so that new land can be created and the rugged individualists—the bandits of agriculture—whose cursed thirst for profit is at the root of the mischief can be given a second chance.

Sometimes we are put into difficulty by the laws of nature, starvation. Just like if you eat more and then next two days you cannot eat; you have to starve. Similarly the difficulty in this material world is that we take more than what we need; therefore we have created problems. Otherwise there is sufficient supply from God's side. There is no scarcity, no problem. We have created problems. Just like in your country sometimes I have heard that you throw away grains, thousands of tons of grains, in the water. That means you have enough food. But there are countries who are starving. So it could be adjusted by sending this food. Instead of throwing in the water, they could be sent to the starving countries. But people will not do that. The point is from God's arrangement, there is enough food within this planet. There is enough land, enough food-producing prospect. But we have arranged in such a way that in one part the people are suffering, and one part, they are throwing the grains in the water. This is not God's arrangement. This is our arrangement. Therefore the problems are created by men. Now the so-called politician, they create problems. Otherwise, by nature's ways, by God's way, everything is complete.

purnam idam purnam adah
purnat purnam udacyate
purnasya purnam adaya
purnam eva avasisyate
[Iso Invocation]
This is Vedic song. God is complete. His creation is complete. His arrangement is complete. Simply we are creating disturbance. Therefore the real education to stop this disturbance is to make people God conscious. Then all problems will be solved. Otherwise, by passing resolution in the United Nations it is not possible.

~ Srila Prabhupada (Sri Brahma-samhita, Lecture -- New York, July 28, 1971)

Nature is anxious to make a new and better start and naturally has no patience with the inefficient. Perhaps when the time comes for a new essay in farming, mankind will have learnt a great lesson—how to subordinate the profit motive to the sacred duty of handing over unimpaired to the next generation the heritage of a fertile soil. *Soil erosion is nothing less than the outward and visible sign of the complete failure of a policy.* The causes of this failure are to be found in ourselves.

The damage already done by soil erosion all over the world looked at in the mass is very great and is rapidly increasing. The regional contributions to this destruction, however, vary widely.

In some areas like north-western Europe, where most of the agricultural land is under a permanent or temporary cover crop (in the shape of grass or leys), and there is still a large area of woodland and forest, soil erosion is a minor factor in agriculture.

In other regions like parts of North America, Africa, Australia, and the countries bordering the Mediterranean, where extensive deforestation has been practised and where almost uninterrupted cultivation has been the rule, large tracts of land once fertile have been almost completely destroyed.

USA

Conservation As A National Agenda

The United States of America is perhaps the only country where anything in the nature of an accurate estimate of the damage done by erosion has been made. Theodore Roosevelt first warned the country as to its national importance. Then came the Great War with its high prices, which encouraged the wasteful exploitation of soil fertility on an unprecedented scale. A period of financial depression, a series of droughts and dust-storms, emphasized the urgency of the salvage of agriculture.

During Franklin Roosevelt's Presidency, soil conservation has become a political and social problem of the first importance. In 1937 the condition and needs of the agricultural land of the U.S.A. were appraised. No less than 253,000,000 acres, or 61 per cent. of the total area under crops, had either been completely or partly destroyed or had lost most of its fertility. Only 161,000,000 acres, or 39 percent of the cultivated area, could be safely farmed by present methods.

In less than a century the United States has therefore lost nearly three-fifths of its agricultural capital. If the whole of the potential resources of the country could be utilized and the best possible practices introduced everywhere, about 447,466,000 acres could be brought into use—an area somewhat greater than the present crop land area of 415,334,931 acres. The position therefore is not hopeless. It will, however, be very difficult, very expensive, and very time consuming to restore the vast areas of eroded land even if money is no object and large amounts of manure are used and green-manure crops are ploughed under.

The root of this soil erosion trouble in the United States is misuse of the land. The causes of this misuse include lack of individual knowledge of soil fertility on the part of the pioneers and their descendants; the traditional attitude which regarded the land as a source of profit; defects in farming systems, in tenancy, and finance—most mortgages contain no provisions for the maintenance of fertility; instability of agricultural production (as carried out by millions of individuals), prices and income in contrast to industrial production carried on by a few large corporations.

The need for maintaining a correct relation between industrial and agricultural production so that both can develop in full swing on the basis of abundance has only recently been understood. The country was so vast, its agricultural resources were so immense, that the profit seekers could operate undisturbed until soil fertility—the country's capital—began to vanish at an alarming rate.

The present position, although disquieting, is not impossible. The resources of the Government are being called up to put the land in order. The magnitude of the effort, the mobilization of all available knowledge, the practical steps that are being taken to save what is left of the soil of the country and to help Nature to repair the damage already done are graphically set out in *Soils and Men*, the Year Book of the United States Department of Agriculture of

1938. This is perhaps the best local account of soil erosion which has yet appeared.

Africa

The rapid agricultural development of Africa was soon followed by soil erosion. In South Africa, a pastoral country, some of the best grazing areas are already semi-desert. The Orange Free State in 1879 was covered with rich grass, interspersed with reedy pools, where now only useless gullies are found. Towards the end of the nineteenth century it began to be realized all over South Africa that serious over-stocking was taking place.

"Snails do a good job of fertilizing the soil, but they're so slow about it."

In 1928 the Drought Investigation Commission reported that soil erosion was extending rapidly over many parts of the Union, and that the eroded material was silting up reservoirs and rivers and causing a marked decrease in the underground water-supplies. The cause of erosion was considered to be the reduction of vegetal cover brought about by incorrect veld management—the concentration of stock in kraals, over-stocking, and indiscriminate burning to obtain fresh autumn or winter grazing.

In Basutoland, a normally well-watered country, soil erosion is now the most immediately pressing administrative problem. The pressure of population has brought large areas under the plough and has intensified over-stocking on the remaining pasture.

In Kenya the soil erosion problem has become serious during the last three years, both in the native reserves and in the European areas. In the former, wealth depends on the possession of large flocks and herds; barter is carried on in terms of live stock; the bride price is almost universally paid in animals; numbers rather than quality are the rule.

The natural consequence is over-stocking, over-grazing, and the destruction of the natural covering of the soil. Soil erosion is the inevitable result. In the European areas erosion is caused by long and continuous overcropping without the adoption of measures to prevent the loss of soil and to maintain the humus content. Locusts have of late been responsible for greatly accelerated erosion; examples are to be seen where the combined effect of locusts and goats has resulted in the loss of a foot of surface soil in a single rainy season.

The countries bordering the Mediterranean provide striking examples of soil erosion, accompanied by the formation of deserts which are considered to be due to one main cause—the slow and continuous deforestation. Originally well wooded, no forests are to be found in the Mediterranean region proper. Most of the original soil has been washed away by the sudden winter torrents.

GLOBAL SOIL SECURITY SYMPOSIUM

Texas A&M University
College Station, Texas, USA
May 19-21 2015

TEXAS A&M
UNIVERSITY
Further details at
soilsecurity.tamu.edu

In North Africa the fertile cornfields, which existed in Roman times, are now desert. Ferrari in his book on woods and pastures refers to the changes in the soil and climate of Persia after its numerous and majestic parks were destroyed; the soil was transformed into sand; the climate became arid and suffocating; springs first decreased and then disappeared.

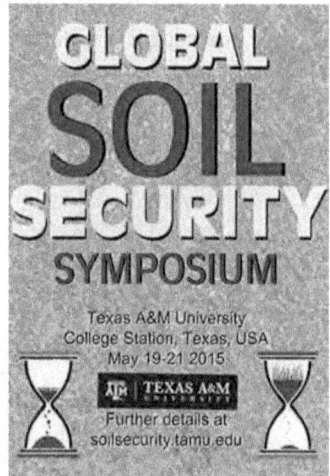

> *"Earth provides enough to satisfy every man's needs, but not every man's greed."*
> ~ *Mahatma Gandhi*

Similar changes took place in Egypt when the forests were devastated; a decrease in rainfall and in soil fertility was accompanied by loss of uniformity in the climate. Palestine was once covered with valuable forests and fertile pastures and possessed a cool and moderate climate; to-day its mountains are denuded, its rivers are almost dry, and crop production is reduced to a minimum.

The above examples indicate the wide extent of soil erosion, the very serious damage that is being done, and the fundamental cause of the trouble—misuse of the land. In dealing with the remedies which have been suggested and which are now being tried out, it is essential to envisage the real nature of the problem. It is nothing less than the repair of Nature's drainage system—the river—and of Nature's method of providing the country-side with a regular water-supply. The catchment area of the river is the natural unit in erosion control. In devising this control we must restore the efficiency of the catchment area as a drain and also as a natural storage of water. Once this is accomplished we shall hear very little about soil erosion.

Reference

The Soil and Health: A Study of Organic Agriculture

An Agricultural Testament - Albert Howard - 10

Farming and Gardening for Health or Disease - Chapter 7

36

Japan

Preventing A National Disaster

Japan provides perhaps the best example of the control of soil erosion in a country with torrential rains, highly erodible soils, and a topography which renders the retention of the soil on steep slopes very difficult. Here erosion has been effectively held in check, by methods adopted regardless of cost, for the reason that the alternative to their execution would be national disaster.

The great danger from soil erosion in Japan is the deposition of soil debris from the steep mountain slopes on the rice-fields below. The texture of the rice soils must be maintained so that the fields will hold water and allow minimum of it through drainage.

If such areas became covered with a deep layer of permeable soil, brought down by erosion from the hill-sides, they would no longer hold water, and rice cultivation—the mainstay of Japan's food-supply—would be out of the question.

For this reason the country has spent as much as ten times the capital value of eroding land on soil conservation work, mainly as an

insurance for saving the valuable rice lands below. Thus in 1925 the Tokyo Forestry Board spent 453 yen (£45) per acre in anti-erosion measures on a forest area, valued at 40 yen per acre, in order to save rice-fields lower down valued at 240 to 300 yen per acre.

The dangers from erosion have been recognized in Japan for centuries and an exemplary technique has been developed for preventing them. It is now a definite part of national policy to maintain the upper regions of each catchment area under forest, as the most economical and effective method of controlling flood waters and insuring the production of rice in the valleys. For many years erosion control measures have formed an important item in the national budget.

According to Lowdermilk, erosion control in Japan is like a game of chess. The forest engineer, after studying his eroding valley, makes his first move, locating and building one or more check dams. He waits to see what Nature's response is.

This determines the forest engineer's next move, which may be another dam or two, an increase in the former dam, or the construction of side retaining walls. After another pause for observation, the next move is made and so on until erosion is checkmated.

The operation of natural forces, such as sedimentation and re-vegetation, are guided and used to the best advantage to keep down costs and to obtain practical results. No more is attempted than Nature has already done in the region. By 1929 nearly 2,000,000 hectares of protection forests were used in erosion control. These forest areas do more than control erosion. They help the soil to absorb and maintain large volumes of rain-water and to release it slowly to the rivers and springs.

Reference

Farming and Gardening for Health or Disease

The Soil and Health: A Study of Organic Agriculture

Sustainable Farming Systems in Upland Areas, ©APO 2004, ISBN: 92-833-7031-7

37

China

A Callous Approach

China, on the other hand, presents a very striking example of the evils which result from the inability of the administration to deal with the whole of a great drainage unit. On the slopes of the upper reaches of the Yellow River extensive soil erosion is constantly going on.

Every year the river transports over 2,000 million tons of soil, sufficient to raise an area of 400 square miles by 5 feet. This is provided by the easily erodible loess soils of the upper reaches of

the catchment area. The mud is deposited in the river bed lower down so that the embankments which contain the stream have constantly to be raised.

Periodically the great river wins in this unequal contest and destructive inundations result. The labour expended on the embankments is lost because the nature of the erosion problem as a whole has not been grasped, and the area drained by the Yellow River has not been studied and dealt with as a single organism.

The difficulty now is the over-population of the upper reaches of the catchment area, which prevents afforestation and laying down of grass. Had the Chinese maintained effective control of the upper reaches—the real cause of the trouble—the erosion problem in all probability would have been solved long ago at a lesser cost in labour than that which has been devoted to the embankment of the river.

China, unfortunately, does not stand alone in this matter. A number of other rivers, like the Mississippi, are suffering from overwork, followed by periodical floods as the result of the growth of soil erosion in the upper reaches.

Although the damage done by uncontrolled erosion all over the world is very great, and the case for action needs no argument, nevertheless there is one factor on the credit side which has been overlooked in the recent literature. A considerable amount of new soil is being constantly produced by natural weathering agencies from the sub-soil and the parent rock. This when suitably conserved will soon re-create large stretches of valuable land.

One of the best regions for the study of this question is the black cotton soil of Central India, which overlies the basalt. Here, although erosion is continuous, the soil does not often disappear altogether, for the reason that as the upper layers are removed by rain, fresh soil is reformed from below.

The large amount of earth so produced is well seen in the Gwalior State, where the late Ruler employed an irrigation officer, lent by the Government of India, to construct a number of embankments, each furnished with spillways, across many of the valleys, which had suffered so badly by uncontrolled rain-wash in the past that they appeared to have no soil at all, the scrub vegetation just managing to survive in the crevices of the bare rock. How great is the annual formation of new soil, even in such unpromising circumstances, must be seen to be believed.

In a very few years, the construction of embankments was followed by stretches of fertile land which soon carried fine crops of wheat. A brief illustrated account of the work done by the late Maharaja of Gwalior would be of great value at the moment for introducing a much needed note of optimism in the consideration of this soil erosion problem.

Why is the forest such an effective agent in the prevention of soil erosion and in feeding the springs and rivers? The forest does two things: (1) the trees and undergrowth break up the rainfall into fine spray and the litter on the ground protects the soil from erosion; (2) the residues of the trees and animal life met with in all woodlands are converted into humus, which is then absorbed by the soil underneath, increasing its porosity and water-holding power.

The soil cover and the soil humus together prevent erosion and at the same time store large volumes of water. These factors—soil protection, soil porosity, and water retention—conferred by the living forest cover, provide the key to the solution of the soil erosion problem.

All other purely mechanical remedies such as terracing and drainage are secondary matters, although of course important in their proper place. The soil must have as much cover as possible; it must be well stocked with humus so that it can drink in and retain the rainfall. It follows, therefore, that in the absence of trees there must be a grass cover, some cover-crop, and ample provision for

keeping up the supply of humus. Each field so provided suffers little or no erosion.

This confirms the view of Williams (Timiriasev Academy, Moscow) who, before erosion became important in the Soviet Union, advanced an hypothesis that *the decay of past civilizations was due to a decline in soil fertility,* consequent on the destruction of the soil's crumb structure when the increasing demands of civilization necessitated the wholesale ploughing up of grass-land.

Williams regarded grass as the basis of all agricultural land utilization and the soil's chief weapon against the plundering instincts of humanity. His views are exerting a marked influence on soil conservation policy in the U.S.S.R. and indeed apply to many other countries.

Grass is a valuable factor in the correct design and construction of surface drains. Whenever possible these should be wide, very shallow, and completely grassed over. The run-off then drains away as a thin sheet of clear water, leaving all the soil particles behind.

The grass is thereby automatically manured and yields abundant fodder. This simple device was put into practice at the Shahjahanpur Sugar Experiment Station in India. The earth service roads and paths were excavated so that the level was a few inches below that of the cultivated area. They were then grassed over, becoming very effective drains in the rainy season, Carrying off the excess rainfalls clear water without any loss of soil.

If we regard erosion as the natural consequence of improper methods of agriculture, and the catchment area of the river as the natural unit for the application of soil conservation methods, the various remedies available fall into their proper place.

The upper reaches of each river system must be afforested; cover crops including grass and leys must be used to protect the arable surface whenever possible; the humus content of the soil must be increased and the crumb structure restored so that each field can drink in its own rainfall; over-stocking and over-grazing must be prevented; simple mechanical methods for conserving the soil and regulating the run-off, like terracing, contour cultivation and contour drains, must be utilized.

There is, of course, no single anti-erosion device which can be universally adopted. The problem must, in the nature of things, be a local one. Nevertheless, certain guiding principles exist which apply everywhere. First and foremost is the restoration and maintenance of soil fertility, so that each acre of the catchment area can do its duty by absorbing its share of the rainfall.

Bibliography

Gorrie, R. M. 'The Problem Of Soil Erosion In The British Empire, With Special Reference To India', Journal Of The Royal Society Of Arts, Lxxxvi, 1938, P. 901.

Howard, Sir Albert. 'A Note On The Problem Of Soil Erosion', Journal Of The Royal Society Of Arts, Lxxxvi, 1938, P. 926.

Jacks, G. V., And Whyte, R. O. Erosion And Soil Conservation, Bulletin 25, Imperial Bureau Of Pastures And Forage Crops, Aberystwyth, 1938.

The Rape Of The Earth: A World Survey Of Soil Erosion, London, 1939.

Soils And Men, Year Book Of Agriculture, 1938, U.S. Dept. Of Agr., Washington,

D.C., 1938.

Alkali Soils

Hilgard, E. W. Soils, New York, 1906.

Howard, A. Crop Production In India, Oxford University Press, 1924.

King, F. H. Irrigation And Drainage, London, 1900.

Ossendowski, F. Man And Mystery In Asia, London, 1924.

Russell, Sir John. Soil Conditions And Plant Growth, London, 1937.

38

One Who Feeds The World

A Victim of Hunger

A Case Study

Farmers all over the world are in a sorry state. Farming, which is called the noblest profession, has lesser takers nowadays. People are shying away from this. This does not bode well for world's food supply. Let us take the example of Punjab (India) which is the bread basket of India.

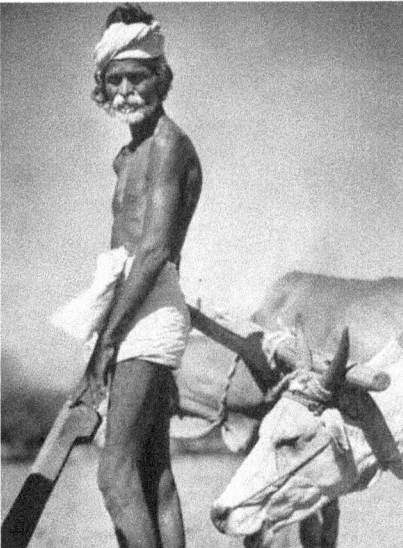

When one thinks of Punjab, one imagines fields of golden wheat and rich farmers. But if we dig a little deeper, we will find that small farmers in the state are caught in the vicious cycle of debt and poverty.

Recently, Indian media highlighted the plight of Punjab's farmers. Harpreet Singh, a farmer's son was quoted as saying, "We want to eat delicious food like kheer and Dal but we don't get it. What we get is only saag. Sometimes we don't even get roti and have to sleep hungry. This happens twice or thrice a month,"

The last time Harpreet tasted kheer (rice and milk pudding) was at a wedding in a Gurdwara, a year ago. And as he spoke, his helpless father Harjit Singh couldn't stop crying. A landless farmer in Sangrur, Harjit managed to lease one acre of land for cultivation.

But while he spent Rs 32,000 on rent and input costs, he earned just Rs 24,000 after selling his crop.

He had to borrow from the local moneylender at an exorbitant rate to make up for his losses. "I am not able to give more than two meals and at times not even that to my family. The produce is poor and if it rains, I can't even work as labourer. How do I earn and feed my family?" says Harjit.

FACTORY FARMERS

Five years ago, Harjit Singh met with an accident. He couldn't afford treatment, leaving his arm deformed. His neighbour Malkiat Singh too can't afford treatment for his eyes even though he runs the risk of turning blind. Being the only earning member in his family, he can't afford a break either. "Doctor says I should get operated or otherwise I will go blind. But I don't have money to even properly feed my family. How do I get operated?" Malkiat said.

For a small farmer, it costs Rs 25,000 to 35,000 to till one acre of land. Input costs are anything between Rs 18,000 to 25,000. Also, the rent on the land ranges from Rs 10,000 to 15,000. So, small farmers often end up paying from his own pocket because he rarely makes a profit and the downturn has made the matters worse.

The standing crop looks beautiful, but the other side of the story -- that of the farmer -- is not that good. The small farmer is still caught in the vicious cycle of poverty and there is little he can do to get out of it. Ironically the one who feeds the world, is himself a victim of poverty and hunger.

At least in India, say, hundred years before, there was no problem for eating, even for the lower class or any... No, there was no... The society was so made, there was no problem. Why fifty years? In 1933 or '36 in Vrndavana somebody wanted milk, some pilgrims amongst ourselves. So went to a house. "Can you supply us some milk?" "Ah, how much you want?" So it was about ten pounds. So she supplied immediately, one woman, and when she was offered price, "Oh, why shall I take a price for ten or twenty pounds of milk? Oh, you can take it." That is my practical experience. Milk was so freely available. So simply we are creating problems by godless civilization. That is a fact.

— Srila Prabhupada (Room Conversation, December 21, 1970, Surat, India)

39

Soil And Climate Change

A Lesson From The Romans

Tom Hodgkinson, 2nd October, 2009

What have the Romans ever done for us? Well, they did at least try to warn us that intensive farming would render our soils and civilisation unviable.

According to the old Roman husbandry writers like Columella and Cato, it's fascinating to note that the Romans, in the later period, had very similar problems to us today, in that they fretted about the depletion of the soil and climate change. Columella, who was a native of Cadiz in Southern Spain, then a Roman colony, wrote his books, very roughly speaking, in the years 50-70 AD, nearly 2,000 years ago. His De Re Rustica (On Agriculture), opens with the following comments:

Again and again I hear leading men of our state condemning now the unfruitfulness of the soil, now the inclemency of the climate for some seasons past, as harmful to crops; and some I hear reconciling the aforesaid complaints, as if on well-founded reasoning, on the ground that, in their opinion, the soil was worn out and exhausted by overproduction of earlier days and can no longer furnish sustenance.

Columella argues that mother earth does not in actual fact become exhausted. It is really a problem of bad stewardship:

> For the matter of husbandry, which all the best of our ancestors had treated with the best of care, we have delivered over to all the worst of our slaves, as if to a hangman for punishment.

Then as now, farms had become enormous factories, with up to 80,000 slaves producing food for the Empire. Elegant Romans had removed themselves from the soil and actually looked down on farming and farmers. This was not the case, says Columella, in the old days, when keeping a smallholding was a noble pursuit:

> We think it beneath us to till our lands with our own hands... but it was a matter of pride with our forefathers to give their attention to farming, from which pursuit came Quinctius Cincinnatus [in 458 BC], summoned from the plough to the dictatorship to be the deliverer of a beleaguered consul and his army, and then, again laying down the power which he relinquished after victory more hastily than he had assumed it for command, to return to the same bullocks and his small ancestral inheritance of four iugera [one iugera was about three fifths of an acre].

Columella also mentions a Roman obesity problem, linked to lazy lifestyles, and criticises, rather like an outraged tabloid newspaper, an over-indulgence in 'drunkenness' and 'gaming':

> The consequence is that ill health attends so slothful a manner of living; for the bodies of our young men are so flabby and enervated that death seems likely to make no change to them.

So Columella, rather like Cobbett in the 19th century, John Seymour in the 20th, and Hugh Fearnley-Whittingstall in our own, sees that the answer to our agricultural problems is to return dignity to the art of husbandry and encourage more people to till the land. We should be doing something useful he says, and we make the mistake of 'plying our hands [ie clapping] in the circuses and theatres rather than in the grainfields and vineyards'.

To this end he wrote twelve books of farming and gardening advice, including many suggestions on how to improve the soil and keep it fertile. He also gives directions on how to look after bees, poultry, pigs, cattle and sheep. Columella's is a hopeful message because it returns power to the people, unlike the limp

The aborigines were in fact far better at maintaining and conserving the central Australian landscapes, the central Australian arid regions, than any Australian since European colonization.

The aborigines lived in almost perfect harmony with their environment for thirty thousand years, thirty to forty thousand recorded years -- that's how far our research can take us back -- whereas in a little over a hundred years, European man in Australia has done in places irreparable damage to not only the vegetation but also the soils of arid Australia. It's damage that will probably never, ever be repaired because the environment is so delicate in central Australia that as soon as our cloven-footed animals, our sheep and our cattle, for example, are brought into the arid areas, they eat, they trample, they remove vegetation. This loosens the soil; the soil is very thin. It's very unfertile, and it blows away. And virtually all you have left is rock. And nothing grows, of course, on rock. That's an over-simplification and perhaps an over-dramatization, but this has happened in Australia. It didn't happen when the aborigines lived here, undisturbed by us. It has happened since European man has come.

In Perth, in this city, around this city, since Europeans have come, we have removed forests, we've cut down trees, we've tilled the soil, we have changed the natural order of things, we have increased the amount of water from rain that flows through the soil. It's getting more and more salty. We are affecting our coastal wetlands, as we call them, the lagoons and the lakes and the marshes, so that they are becoming both more salty and more clogged with silt and soil and debris. Water birds can, in some areas, no longer live there. Fish are dying. A lot of migratory fish and crabs, for example, are no longer migrating to their traditional breeding grounds.

We're stuck with that... Whether we like it or not, we're stuck with our urban civilization. We're stuck with our Western way of doing things, unfortunately. ~Justin Murphy, Geographer (Conversation with Srila Prabhupada, May 14, 1975, Perth)

and ultimately profitless strategy of trying to persuade a capitalist government to change people's ways by force and persuasion. What is astonishing really is how close Columella's advice is to what you might find in a contemporary book about organic gardening or Permaculture. Climate change is clearly nothing new:

I have found many authorities now worthy of remembrance were convinced that with the long wasting of the ages, weather and climate undergo a change... that regions which formerly, because of the unremitting severity of winter, could not safeguard any shoot of the vine or the olive planted in them, now that the earlier coldness has abated and the weather is becoming more clement, produce oil harvests and the vintages of Bacchus in the greatest abudance.

The Roman Empire was to last another four hundred years or so after Columella was writing. It would seem that the answer to soil exhaustion and climate change is the same as it has ever been: simply to get back to the land.

40

Vital Role Of Cattle Manure

In Maintaining Soil's Organic Matter

William A. Albrecht, PhD

The use of "fossil" fuels in their various forms, like coal, kerosene, gasoline, and other volatile, readily combustible materials for agricultural power, to replace that of horses and mules, has brought about the highly exploitative attacks on the natural reserve organic matter of our surface soils.

This has resulted for two reasons: (a) more power and speed are applied to the tilling of the soil more deeply and vigorously to hasten the combustion of the reserves of microbial energy materials; (b) less organic matter is returned in the animal feed residues as manure, modified and improved as nutrition for the soil microbes and plants by the addition of the chemically more complex and varied waste products of the animal's physiology.

Reasons

The first of these reasons has been widely recognized as an unavoidable result of the high labor costs demanding such speed to raise the output per man.

The second reason has been generally disregarded. Manure handling has always been considered a distasteful sanitary chore incidental to keeping animals housed and penned, more than it

Striking Results . . . Farm manure (six tons per acre annually — right) demonstrated its effects (July, 1958) in the upkeep of soil productivity under corn continuously (69th successive crop) in contrast to that of the soil under similar cropping but no manure (left). The same noble hybrid seed on both plots didn't overcome the difference in the soils due to manure and no manure.

has been appreciated as an essential, biochemical contribution to the nutritional quality of feeds and foods grown on manured soil. Also, it simultaneously does much to maintain the organic matter in its fertilizing services.

Chemical studies were made of the soils after 67 years of (a) no cattle manure on one set of plots, and (b) six tons per acre annually on another. Each set in such contrasting pairs had been under cropping to (a) wheat, (b) corn, (c) timothy annually, and also to (d) a four-year rotation of corn, oats, wheat, and clover, and (e) a six-year rotation of corn, oats, wheat, clover and timothy. From these data, it is clearly evident how much the use of barnyard manure (cow dung) has contributed to help in the upkeep of the organic matter supply in those soils. (See the table).

Results

Under cropping to wheat continuously, the manured plot of soil had 2.4 percent of organic matter, when the unmanured one had only 2.1 percent. The former was three parts richer over 21 parts, or higher by one-seventh. Under corn continuously, the manure plot was higher in organic matter after the 67 years by four-sevenths. Under timothy sod continuously, the increase figure was nearly one-

Soil Composition--Due to Barnyard Manure after 67 Years. Sanborn Field. Columbia, Missouri

Crop	Treatment	Organic Matter %	Phosphoric Acid. lbs/A	Essential M.E. Ca	Cations Exchangeable Mg	Cations Exchangeable K	Cation Exchange Capacity M.E.	Hydrogen M.E.
Wheat	Manure	2.4	189	2140	306	348	16	8.5
Wheat	None	2.1	77	1900	360	312	16	9.5
Corn	Manure	2.2	202	3350	565	414	17	6.0
Corn	None	1.4	62	2600	462	239	15	8.0
Timothy	Manure	3.0	201	2650	216	273	15	4.9
Timothy	None	2.3	15	2100	140	144	15	4.8
4-year Rotation	Manure	2.7	151	3850	245	307	18	4.8
4-year Rotation	None	2.0	38	3230	245	307	18	4.8
6-year Rotation	Manure	2.5	94	2600	210	233	16	4.5
6-year Rotation	None	2.0	22	2866	108	113	16	4.6

third; under the four year rotation, it was over one-third; and in the six-year rotation, one-fourth, or next to the lowest, which was the soil under wheat. These were the effects from using manure when in all of these cases the entire crops had been removed and no crop residues were returned.

Help From Cattle Manure

As additional significance, there is the help from barnyard manure in the maintenance of the inorganic part of the soil fertility. This was shown by the ash analysis of the soil for phosphate (phosphoric acid, P2O5) and for some of the cationic essential elements, namely: calcium, Ca; magnesium, Mg; and potassium, K.

It is also significant to note the help from manure in keeping up the soil's exchange--absorption capacity (cation exchange capacity), in which the organic matter is more active than the clay. Also the lowered soil acidity resulting from the use of manure, as measured by the amount of exchangeable hydrogen, in the soil after 67 years, deserves attention as a modified soil condition not commonly appreciated in connection with this soil treatment.

Contrasting values in each of the above cases of the elements cited for manure and no manure (Table) show clearly that manure has fertility values we do not commonly emphasize.

Demonstration

After nearly three score and ten years of manuring, this treatment demonstrates that, in the matter of soil maintenance, cattle manure has values for:

(a) upkeep of the supply of reserve organic matter;

(b) holding up the soil's content of phosphorus even when manure is relatively low as a fertilizer for this essential element;

(c) preserving the supply of active potassium;

(d) maintaining the exchangeable magnesium;

(e) preserving the supply of active calcium; and

(f) helping to hold down the excessive concentration of acidity as hydrogen.

Manuring the soil has been doing these things for years under merely the belief in it as a good practice, and long before science gave us these few tabulations of what we can prove in favor of cattle manure. In the organic matter of the soil as part of the nutrition of microbes, plants, animals and man there is still much in the realm of good practice and much remains yet for science to prove and to explain.

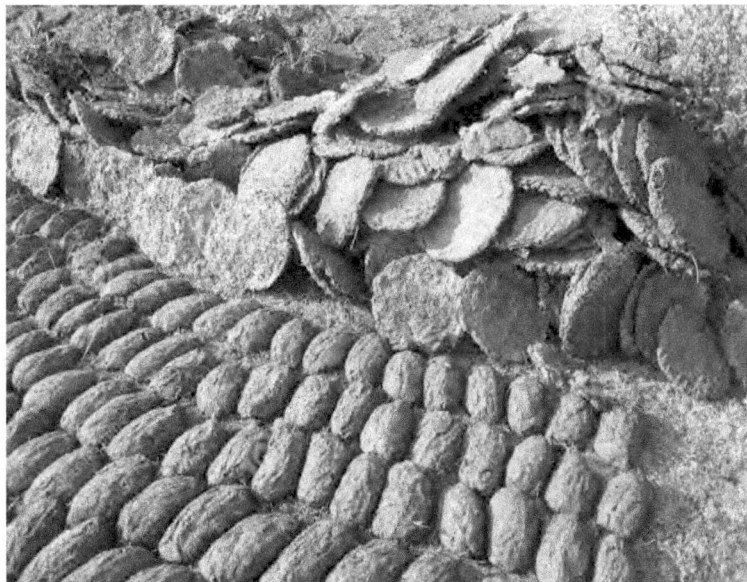

Respect For Nature

The facts that have been outlined will be observed in nature by those who do not have preconceived ideas about plant growth. Unfortunately the professional agriculturalist often views the effects of soils on the plant's growth with a distant outlook, as if the only problems were those of industrial manipulation of dead materials, with emphasis on the various technologies for economic advantages only.

People who approach agricultural research in this way have lost sight of agriculture as a biological demonstration by the forces of nature, *where man is more spectator than manager in complete control of soil and produce.*

Such unrealistic views of agriculture have led to expressions and views by high government officials that soil is but a chemical and physical agent for the production of larger quantities of crops. They seem unaware that the soil of our planet is a complex material developed through many centuries, having the power of creation, not only for plants, but for everything that lives, moves and has its being upon the earth.

(William A. Albrecht, Phd, 1888–1974, was the Chairman of Department of Soils, College of Agriculture, University of Missouri, Columbia.)

41

Organic Matter In Soil

Best Defense Against Erosion And Water Shortages

By Donald P. Hopkins

O rganic matter in soil can absorb and store much more water than can inorganic fractions. It acts like a sponge, taking up water and releasing it as required by plants. It also helps bind soil particles into larger aggregates, or crumbs. Soils with this kind of structure are very resistant to erosion. Conversely, nearly all soils containing little or no organic matter are very susceptible to erosion.

Besides absorbing water readily, a good cropland soil should be able to dry out or warm up quickly when the rain is over. It should hold enough moisture to supply the needs of a crop between rains, yet permit water to pass through the soil. A good soil will not stay too wet or too dry.

"A governmental policy which results in impoverishing the natural fertility of land, no matter by what particular name it is called must have an end. It is only a question of time when this truly spendthrift course, this abuse of the goodness of Providence, shall meet its inevitable punishment.

Down to this day, great cities have ever been the worst desolators of the earth. It is for this that they have been so frequently buried many feet beneath the rubbish of their idols of brick, stone, and mortar, to be exhumed in after ages. . . . Their inhabitants violated the laws of nature which govern the health of man and secure the enduring productiveness of the soil.

There are other, less obvious relationships between soil erosion and crop selection and management. Many soils can be planted with maize without much erosion risk if the maize crop is rotated with legumes and small grains. If maize is planted year after year, however, soil losses begin to mount.

42

Earthworm - Our True Friend

Cattle Manure Is Earthworm Friendly And Chemical Fertilizers Destroy Them

Donald P. Hopkins (Chemicals, Humus And The Soil)

When we come to the larger soil organisms, and in particular to the earthworm, the humus school stands in a stronger position. For the earthworm's contribution to soil fertility has been sadly neglected by modern soil science. Even in the United States where official research facilities in agriculture are so liberally supported, even there most of the modern work upon the earthworm has been left in private hands.

The scientific estimation of the earthworm's contribution begins with Charles Darwin. Over a number of years he observed worms' habits and the many kinds of soil changes they brought about, and in 1881 he published a monograph, The Formation of Vegetable Mould Through the Action of Worms with Observations on Their Habits.

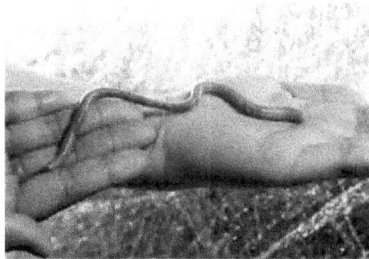

This exhaustive study was no ordinary record of a naturalist's investigation, otherwise there might be more excuse for the scanty attention paid to it by contemporary and later science. Darwin was not content to present a 'purist' view of the worm—he went much beyond this and stressed the important consequences of worms' habits to the soil. But what should have been a classic in scientific literature caused practically no stir at all. Darwin's fame was to rest upon apes, not worms.

In 1945, however, and in no small measure due to the activity of the modern humus school, this book was republished under the neater title, Darwin on Humus and the Earthworm (Faber and Faber), with a preface by Sir Albert Howard. Not unnaturally Sir Albert tied up

The charge that chemical fertilizers are a prime cause of unhealthy growth is shown by the following quotations:

'Diseases are on the increase. With the spread of artificials and the exhaustion of the original supplies of humus carried by every fertile soil, there has been a corresponding increase in the diseases of crops and animals which feed upon them.'

~Sir Albert Howard, An Agricultural Testament.

'My canes (raspberry) have not had any chemical fertilizers, and in consequence have not required spraying. In this, as in other cases, no chemicals means no sprays.'

~F. C. King, article in The Market Grower, 18.3.44.

'The accelerated growth induced by chemical fertilizers has the effect, among others, of speeding up the rate at which humus is exhausted. As this depletion of humus proceeded, troubles began. Parasites and diseases appeared in the crops, and epidemics became rife among our livestock, so that poison sprays and sera had to be introduced to control these conditions.'

~E. B. Balfour, The Living Soil.

'Now sulphate of ammonia and many other artificial manures are likely to kill the earthworm and bacterial life of the soil, and so one gets ill-nourished plants which are liable to fatal attack by disease and insect pests. Disease, fungus, and insect pests are always with us, but they chiefly affect the unhealthy plant.'

~Lord Lymington, Famine in England.

Darwin's neglected points with the humus school thesis. But before we inquire into this enrolment of Darwin as a member of the humus school—or should it be as a distinguished past-president?—it is best to see what Darwin himself said.

Haven't seen you around here before.

Don't be silly. I'm your other end.

Apart from a large number of brilliant deductions about the way worms live, Darwin proved that they eat raw and half-decayed organic matter and also pass through their bodies considerable quantities of earth. In this intermingling process they produce a rich vegetable mould or well-humified soil, and this is constantly being added to the upper surface of soils.

To quote the original monograph: 'Worms have played a more important part in the history of the world than most persons would at first suppose. In almost all humid countries they are extraordinarily numerous, and for their size possess great muscular power. In many parts of England a weight of more than ten tons of dry earth annually passes through their bodies and is brought to the surface of each acre of land; so that the whole superficial bed of vegetable mould passes through their bodies in the course of every few years. . . .'

And again: 'Worms prepare the ground in an excellent manner for the growth of fibrous-rooted plants and for seedlings of all kinds. They periodically expose the mould to the air, and sift it so that no stones larger than they can swallow are left in it. They mingle the whole together, like a gardener who prepares fine soil for his choicest plants.'

'In this state it is well fitted to retain moisture and to absorb all soluble substances, as well as for the process of nitrification. . . .'

As the figure of ten tons per year per acre may seem surprising, it might be as well to summarize the evidence upon which Darwin based this estimate. He was led to believe that the weight of soil normally brought to the surface by worms was fairly high from studying the rate at which large objects such as big stones or even

The Cattle Compost Factory

The compost factory at Indore adjoins the cattle shed. This latter has been constructed for forty oxen and is provided with a cubicle, in which a supply of powdered urine earth can conveniently be stored. The cattle stand on earth. A paved floor is undesirable as the animals rest better, are more comfortable and are warmer on an earthen floor. The earth on which the cattle stand absorbs the urine, and is replaced by new earth to a depth of six inches every three or four months. The compost factory itself is a very simple arrangement. It consists of thirty-three pits, each 30 ft. by 14 ft. and 2 ft. deep with sloping sides, arranged in three rows with sufficient space between the lines of pits for the easy passage of loaded carts. The pits themselves are in pairs, with a space 12 ft. wide between each pair. This arrangement enables carts to be brought up to any particular pit. Ample access from the compost factory to the main roads is also necessary, so that during the carting of the compost to the fields, loaded and empty carts can easily pass one another, and also leave room for the standing carts which are being filled.

Manurial Value Of Indore Compost

One-cart load of Indore compost is equivalent, as regards nitrogen content, to two cart-loads of ordinary farmyard manure. Properly made compost has another great advantage over ordinary manure, namely its fine powdery character which enables it to be uniformly incorporated with the soil and to be rapidly converted into food materials for the crop. Taking everything into consideration, Indore compost has about three times the value of ordinary manure.

~ By Sir Albert Howard, (An Agricultural Testament)

old ruins were gradually buried in the land. He himself and one or two interested friends collected and weighed all the worm castings over timed periods on measured areas of land, on very small plots of about one square yard or so. If the areas were indeed rather tiny, on the other hand the time period was long; but in any case the run of various results was reasonably consistent.

Darwin was able to check the reliability of these figures by approaching the same problem in a different way.

An American measurement, quoted by Sir Albert Howard, shows that the soil of the castings is very much richer than the corresponding soil.

The point that Darwin made verbally in 1881 is thus well and truly confirmed by these 1942 figures from Connecticut Experiment Station.

There may have been other similar measurements in the interim but, if so, little attention has been paid to them. 1881 to 1942 is a long time, and the humus school can well claim in this matter that 'official' research has largely ignored a known biological factor in soil fertility - earthworms.

With this point behind them the humus school has launched a strong attack at chemical fertilizers on the grounds that these materials discourage earthworms, drive them away and thus greatly diminish their powerful contributions. Where chemical fertilizers are used the earthworm populations are low or nil; additional supplies of chemical NPK are then needed to make up for the supplies from the soil's store that would otherwise have been made available by the worms.

The Importance Of Farmyard Dung

In The Beginning Days, Even Fertilizer Companies Admitted It

Donald P. Hopkins (Chemicals Humus, And The Soil)

It is often said that those who have chemicals to sell have harnessed science to their own interests rather than to the interests of the soil.

That is to say, they have paid chemists to concentrate upon the kinds of research that deal with the effects of chemicals whilst nobody else has been very ready or able to foot the bill for scientific inquiries in other directions. It is also often said that the advertising pressure of large chemical firms over-accentuates the favourable claims of chemicals, and this has in a long period led to an unbalanced fashion for chemicals even among scientists themselves.

A kind of fixed-idea-mentality has been built up. From my own contacts with people who directly live by the soil and its produce, I

very much doubt whether there could be any kind of humanity less susceptible either to subtle or crude advertising.

Suspicion and scepticism go hand in hand with the plough and the harvester.

Here are extracts from pre-war literature issued for sales-purposes by one of the largest chemical companies and fertilizer manufacturers in Britain.

When writing the original edition of this book, I made a survey of the sales-literature this company had issued, though it was admittedly limited to the amount that still remained intact and could be gathered together during the war period. I was anxious to check whether charges of chemical bias, and in particular the advocating of using fertilizers to the exclusion of manures, could be substantiated. I found that

The prosecution states that plants raised with chemicals are less robust, less able to withstand the attacks of fungi, pests, and viruses; so that epidemic ill health results. This being so, extra yields are short-term and illusory benefits, quantity and not quality, and quantity in any case that must be frequently discounted by severe loss.

The humus school have suggested why this happens, and we have already analysed some of their evidence for specific charges against chemicals in chapter eleven. But details hardly matter—a fact is still a fact whether it can be explained or not. And we should be able to decide whether the use of fertilizers has increased diseases and attacks by pests—it is the kind of thing that can be assessed reasonably well by observation and measurement; in the widest sense, indeed, by mass observation and statistics.

~ Donald P. Hopkins

on the contrary the complementary use of manure and fertilizers had often been strongly advised.

'The most successful potato growers manure their crops with dung and complete fertilizers.'

'Fertilizers will help to restore exhausted grasses to vigour, but cannot give their full effect unless the pasture is rested at the right time and is therefore in a fit condition to respond.'

'In every country where sugar beet is cultivated, it has been found both essential and profitable to manure the land well with dung and a complete fertilizer.'

'The best rule for the amateur to follow is to apply as much dung as he can get in order to improve the physical condition of his soil, and to make up for any lack of plant-food by the use of other organic and artificial fertilizers.'

'It is not possible to grow well-developed healthy plants with the aid of nitrogen exclusively, whether it be applied in the form of sulphate of ammonia or any other purely nitrogenous fertilizer ... sulphate of ammonia should be used in conjunction with fertilizers supplying phosphates and potash. . . . Supplement your work of cultivation by

A good deal of compost has been made on tea-estates in North India, where the necessary vegetable matter is easily collected from the uncultivated land near the estates. The collection of this material has, however, in places led to bad soil erosion.

'It is stated that the results are best when sufficient quantities of cattle or other animal manure are available; they are said to be less satisfactory where the animal manure has been deficient. Attempts to run tea estates on compost alone, however, proved unsatisfactory; it was necessary to provide the proper artificials where ever sufficient cattle manure was lacking.

~ Sir Albert Howard

conserving all the trimmings from your garden, all lawn mowings, hedge clippings, dead plants, and the like, in a compost heap.'

'Fertility depends on light and air; on methods of cultivation; on the presence in the soil of water; organic matter (humus); of bacteria; of

FARMYARD *We'll help you grow!*
ORGANICS

Weed-Free, Odour-free all-natural Compost

Suppliers of: Compost, Potting Mix, Mulch, Lawn Dressing, Seedling-Growing Medium

nitrogen, phosphates, potash, calcium; and of small quantities of what are known as the minor elements. All these factors are interrelated so that all must be maintained at the right level if fertility is not to suffer.'

None of these quotations was printed in any lesser type than the type in the rest of the general statement. By way of history, here are extracts from a very old-established fertilizer manufacturers' guide for farmers issued as long ago as 1857.

'Judiciously applied, in agriculture, artificial manures meet the natural deficiency of valuable fertilizing constituents in farmyard manures, and when both kinds are used conjointly (which we always recommend when practicable) the value of dung is greatly enhanced.'

'And it should always be borne in mind that these (artificial) manures are intended to supply any deficiency in quantity or quality of farmyard dung, and not to supersede its use.'

Importance Of Humus In Soil Preservation

And Role Of Cow Dung In Humus creation

Humus is a word that was invented before the days of Liebig to cover up a large number of complexities that could not be simplified, and the word remains because the situation also remains. We are still very much in the dark about the precise composition of humus and exactly why it is so important.

However, evidence that comes from observing effects must not be rated lower in value than evidence that can explain the effects. To take up again the analogy of the trial for murder; if a witness is produced who saw the accused stick a knife into the victim, that evidence—provided the witness is reliable—outweighs all the circumstantial evidence that tries to show why the accused had reason to commit the murder or how he had the opportunity and so on.

Humus is the dark brown or black decomposed organic matter invariably noticeable in what are called rich soils. Farmyard manure, stable manure, vegetable waste matter, these in their fresh forms are not humus but rather the raw materials that can be turned into humus.

Properties of Humus

By far the simplest way to interpret humus is to list the things it can do. Its properties—from the point of view of soil fertility—can be divided into three classes; mechanical or physical, biological, and chemical.

The physical or mechanical effects are as follows. It can bind together a light, crumbling soil; but it can also make a sticky, heavy soil more friable.

The erosion disasters in the United States, in which thousands of crop-producing acres became a desert or 'dust-bowl', are now generally admitted to have been caused by humus deficiency. The soils were originally very rich; they were farmed without attention to

Mulch   Compost   Humus

humus replacement—the top-soils became more and more friable, crumbled into dry dust; then, once a certain level in deterioration was reached, nothing could save the soils from being swept away by rough weather.

Humus keeps the soil particles apart and so keeps air moving through the soil. It holds water better than soil so that plants in a humus-rich soil are less affected by drought conditions.

'Humus is a natural body; it is a composite entity, just as are plant, animal, and microbial substances; it is even more complex chemically, since all these materials contribute to its formation.'
~ S. A. Waksman

Sir John Russell has reported that plots at Rothamsted regularly treated with farmyard manures contain 3 to 4 per cent more water than plots under similar cropping conditions but which receive non-humus containing manures. And, of course, every gardener knows how much better are his moisture-needing summer crops like beans, peas, tomatoes, marrows, etc., if rotted organic matter is trenched in underneath them.

A minor physical effect comes from its colour, for by tending to darken the soil it increases the absorption capacity of the soil for warm sun rays and thus can keep the soil temperature a little higher.

Its biological properties are vital. It increases the activities of so many organisms whose work is a favourable factor to soil fertility. From the earthworm to the invisible earth bacteria, the life of the soil population is stimulated by the presence of humus. This is an important matter that we shall have to consider in much more detail later—for the moment let it be left at that.

Chemically, humus—or at any rate the manures that contain humus—will contain supplies of the elements of plant-growth. This is obvious for the manures have been produced by the 'rotting' of plant material——whether a cow has eaten, digested, and expelled

grass or mangolds or whether waste green material has been directly composted in a heap.

At this preliminary and general stage, we need not go into the question of how much of the original minerals etc. taken from the soil by the plants will still remain in the humus type manures which are later put back into the soil; but clearly the manures will have some definite value of this kind.

Also, in this plant food department of soil fertility, humus plays an indirect role; for it can increase the soil's capacity for retaining soluble (and therefore active) kinds of these plant-foods. As we shall see later, there is always a tendency for immediate fertility in soils to be lost through the soil's inability to hold all its active plant-food supply indefinitely. So that the help of humus in compensating for this adverse factor is important.

Humus Creation

How can the humus content of the soil be kept up? By the digging or ploughing in of animal manures—farmyard, stable, or sewage manures. By composting all organic wastes. By the deliberate growing of what are called 'green manure' crops, e.g. mustard, for digging in.

And by the digging in of all crop wastes left after harvesting, e.g. stubble, mangold tops, and so on. When grassland is converted to arable land, as has happened so widely in

If your energy is all engaged in manufacturing tires and wheels, then who will go to the farm...So gradually farming will be reduced, and the city residents, they are satisfied if they can eat meat. And the farmer means keeping the, raising the cattle and killing them, send to the city, and they will think that "We are eating. What is the use of going to..." But these rascals have no brain that "If there is no food grain or grass, how these cattle will be...?" Actually it is happening. They are eating swiftly.

-Srila Prabhupada (Room Conversation with Dr. Theodore Kneupper — November 6, 1976, Vrndavana)

wartime, the turned-in turf provides valuable humus as it slowly rots down in the soil.

It will be noted that the application of fertilizers has not been given as a direct method of providing humus, but the application of bulky organic manures is. This is a fundamental distinction.

Larger crops mean bigger residues for ploughing-back, and also bigger root systems left in the soil to rot down into humus. The extent to which the below-ground parts of crops provide humus is much under-estimated. When a ley is ploughed in, we realize obviously enough that its green stem and foliage matter must make a big contribution to the soil's humus; but the thick mass of root systems underneath may well make an even bigger one.

Farmyard Manure Vs Fertilizer

The difference between farmyard manures and fertilizers is confused by the fact that the manures contain not only humus but also supplies of the fertility elements. In this latter sense, therefore, they overlap the function of fertilizers. We must neither exaggerate the value of this overlap, nor underestimate it.

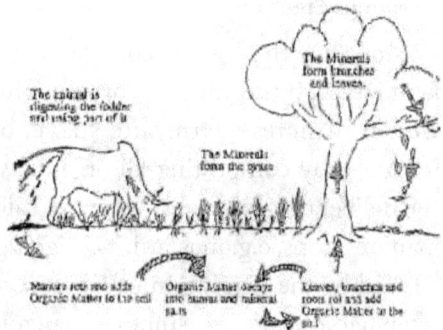

Important questions affecting the whole argument about fertilizers are: (1) how much 'chemical' plant-food do these natural manures provide; (2) how much natural manure of all kinds is, or can

'The fixation of nitrogen is vital to the progress of civilized humanity, and unless we can class it among the certainties to come, the great Caucasian race will cease to be foremost in the world, and will be squeezed out of existence by the races to whom wheaten bread is not the staff of life.'
~ Sir William Crookes, 1898.

be made, available; (3) how much plant-food must be added to the soil to maintain fertility at the level necessary for our requirements?

It is the chemical plant-foods with which fertilizers are more concerned. Liebig made the point that any element found by analysis in the composition of a healthy plant was ipso facto an element necessary to its proper growth. (It is not so true in a quantitative sense, for an element that is present in large quantities in a plant may not be any more important than one present only in very much smaller quantities. The different elements have different functions. One element may function as a direct food; another may be needed only in traces in order to allow the plant to digest the first element.)

The elements found in plants generally are: carbon, nitrogen, hydrogen, oxygen, phosphorus, potassium, calcium, magnesium, sulphur, iron, manganese, chlorine, boron. Even this is not a complete list but it contains the main ones and some minor ones.

Now of these elements there are three important ones that the soil itself does not seem able to supply sufficiently for our cropping needs—nitrogen, phosphorus, and potassium. Each harvested crop takes away supplies of these elements that have come from the soil and, after a time, these losses reduce the soil's ability to go on feeding crops.

By sampling and analysis it is a simple matter for a chemist to measure just how much of these elements is removed, say, per acre by a crop.

Thus, a good crop of potatoes might take from the soil about 150 pounds of potash (oxide of potassium) per acre. What happens to this 150 pounds? The potatoes are eaten, digested, expelled from the human system into the sewage system. In a modern city this usually means that the sewage is treated and then conducted into a river or sea as quietly and unobtrusively as possible. That part of the potash in the discarded peelings may go on to a compost heap or be fed to pigs or poultry in which case a fraction of the potash will eventually find its way back to the soil. But, in sewage disposal, most of the potash is lost completely.

Admitted, there is some sewage reclamation carried on, but it must be remembered that sewage in modern sanitation is heavily diluted with water and this means that the active plant-food—the kind that can dissolve in water-must pass into the liquid fraction of sewage. And it is this liquid fraction that is discarded in most systems—the sludges that are reclaimed at some works are composed of the solid, insoluble parts of sewage. There is, therefore, continuous loss. In less civilized countries—or perhaps it is fairer to say less industrialized countries— the sewage is disposed of by putting it directly back on to and into the soil.

In cattle farming, the nitrogen, phosphorus, and potash consumed when the cattle eat grass or fodder crops returns to the farm as manure. That is why the farmyard manures have been valued so much in traditional farming.

45

Cow Dung

Restoring Lands And Healing Hearts

In India's Conflict Zones

India has a total of 671 districts and out of these, 82 districts are severely affected by Maoist insurgency. These insurgents practically control these vast swathes of territories and even security forces have a hard time accessing some of these areas.

Collapsed agriculture and soil erosion is responsible, in no small measure, for the rise of inurgency in these areas. The youth often have no means of livelihood other than joining the rebel ranks.

One such district in Central India's Chhattisgarh state is Kanker. Most of the land here is degraded and agriculture is in shambles.

Government Projects Facing Reistance

In 2010, the government launched an 820 crore rupee ($140 million) initiative to develop the district. This included building roads, supplying electricity and drinking water, building schools and community health centres and implementing the Mahatma Gandhi National Rural Employment Guarantee Act (MNREGA), a programme designed to end rural poverty by giving 100 days employment a year to the rural poor.

The plan faced stiff opposition from Maoist activists, who said it would only lead to displacement of local tribal people and fill up the pockets of corrupt government officials.

Kalavati Salam, a resident, recalls how Maoists disrupted a government project in 2010. "We brought in trucks full of stone chips, cement and sand to build a tar road. But when the bulldozers came, they set them afire. We had to stop the work and couldn't spend the budget allocated for the project."

A half-built archway at the village entrance, together with heaps of stone and concrete on the roadsides, back up her testimony.

Maya Kavde, head of Makdi Khuna, another village in the same district, says suspected Maoist activists recently vandalised a mobile phone tower in her village by cutting wires and pulling apart the antennas.

Four years after Kalavati Salam was elected to lead the Nangarbeda village council in Central India's Chhattisgarh state, she has finally got her first development plan rolling.

The plan, focused on reversing land degradation and boosting crop yields, benefits from a generous budget and a dedicated work force. Equally important, it has the support of the Communist Party of India (Maoist), a banned political organisation that has blocked many previous development efforts.

When we examine the facts, we must put the Northern Indian cultivator down as the most economical farmer in the world as far as the utilization of the potent element of fertility—nitrogen—goes. In this respect he is more skilful than his Canadian brother. He cannot take a heavy overdraft of nitrogen from the soil. He has only the small current account provided by the few pounds annually added by nature, yet he raises a crop of wheat on irrigated land in the United Provinces that is not far removed from the Canadian average. He does more with a little nitrogen than any farmer I ever heard of. We need not concern ourselves with soil deterioration in these provinces. The present standard of fertility can be maintained indefinitely.

~ Sir Albert Howard (The Waste Products Of Agriculture And Their Utilization As Humus)

"Now we are taking up works like restoring village land. We are trying to change the definition of development," she adds, visibly relieved.

The process includes levelling the land, clearing it of stones, and then covering it with cow dung.

"Most of the farm plots here are uneven, lifeless. We remove layers of soil from those plots that are higher, until the entire farm is at the same level," says villager Sonkumari Bai, 42. "We also remove big and small stones. Sometimes we winnow the top soil before putting it back into the land. *Finally, we till the land and cover it with dried cow dung and gypsum."*

The inhabitants of Nangarbeda, which has a population of 2,700, hope this will help improve their harvests.

"The temperature here is increasing day by day. Earlier in the summer, we would grow vegetables like cucumbers and cow beans. But now the land is so dry, we can grow nothing," says Bhagobai Pradhan, who has a three-acre farm. "This treatment has made some difference. When the rain comes, the once-tilled land will get soaked easily and the cow dung will mix with it well."

Nanak Baghel, a senior Maoist leader in Kanker, says his party fully supports the land restoration project.

"We are against the government-backed so called development projects that are just tools to systematically destroy the tribal people.

But we never oppose people's right to better land, water or forest," says Baghel, an area commander.

Sukhanti Bai, head of Handitola village in another conflict-affected district, Rajnandgaon, describes how soil degradation and falling yields have pushed villagers to restore their land too.

"There are many companies here mining for iron ore and limestone. They have caused a lot of deforestation. Also security forces cut many trees to build their camps inside forests. Now, we

"The philosophy for improving or restoring the environment used to be, remove humans, leave it alone and the land will go back to nature," said environmental activist and author Dan Dagget.

The problem with removing people and their food-producing activities from the land, he says, is that "humans are an important part of the very ecosystems we're trying to restore.

"Removing ourselves from (the landscape) dooms us," he said. "It's like trying to put back together an extremely complex puzzle with a very important piece missing—us."

have less rain and a lot of dust coming from the mines and damaging our fields," she explains.

"Everyone in my village is experiencing a 10 to 20 percent drop in rice yield. Last year, we held a meeting to discuss what work we must make a priority, and everyone said it should be land restoration," she adds.

The majority of the local people are landless, marginal farmers who own less than 2.5 acres of land.

According to Luc Gnacadja, executive secretary of the United Nations Convention to Combat Desertification (UNCCD), including land in development plans will help nations fight food insecurity. "Avoiding land degradation and restoring degraded land should be a centrepiece to every state's development plans," Gnacadja said in a recent interview.

For local people, the land restoration projects in these villages are not only a step towards ensuring food supplies. They also create a more secure working environment.

Ramulu Amma, a 32-year-old villager in Peda Bandirevu, says she feels safer now. We are working to improve our own fields and there are no feelings of fear or insecurity now.

Source

Report, Stella Paul, Reuters, 7 May 2013.

46

Cow Dung Farming

All You Need Is One Cow And Zero Cash

Zero Budget Natural Farming (ZBNF) or holistic agriculture is a method of agriculture that counters the commercial expenditure and market dependency of farmers for the inputs like fertilisers and pesticides.

The method involves locally obtainable natural bio-degradable materials like cow dung and urine and combine scientific knowledge of ecology and modern technology with traditional farming practices based on naturally occurring biological processes.

Zero budget farming methods are promoted by agri-scientists like Subash Palekar and Masanobu Fukuoka.

It requires absolutely no monetary investment for purchase of key inputs like seeds, fertilizers and plant protection chemicals from the market. The farmer can grow hardy local varieties of crops without application of fertilizers and pesticides. Since it is a zero budget farming, no institutional credit would be required and dependence on hired labour is also reduced to bare minimum.

The whole philosophy behind this system is to make the farmer self-reliant so that he is not subjected to volatile market forces.

All that the system requires is a native breed of cow which in any case forms an integral part of farming in India's rural areas. It is claimed that one cow is sufficient to take up this method of farming on thirty acres of land.

Soil Is A Prefect And Complete System

Zero Budget Farming works on the premise that soil is a complete system in itself, independent and self-sustaining. Soil is

om purnam adah purnam idam
purnat purnam udacyate
purnasya purnam adaya
purnam evavasisyate
"The Personality of Godhead is perfect and complete, and because He is completely perfect, all emanations from Him, such as this phenomenal world, are perfectly equipped as complete wholes. Whatever is produced of the complete whole is also complete in itself. Because He is the complete whole, even though so many complete units emanate from Him, He remains the complete balance."
~ *Sri Isopanisad*

perfectly capable of supporting life without any need for artificial inputs or technologies.

How much nutrients the crops takes from the soil? Only 1.5 to 2.0 % Remaining 98 to 98.5% nutrients are taken from air, water and Sun. Every green leaf is a food producing factory. It takes carbon dioxide & nitrogen from the air, water from the clouds and light from the Sun. Every green leaf produces 4.5 gram carbohydrates per square feet surface, from which we get 1.5 gram grains or 2.25 gram fruits. Neither air, nor cloud or Sun send us any bill for their contribution. All these inputs are available free of cost.

Green leaves do not use the technology of the Agriculture Universities or multinational food companies. Neither do the Sun, Moon, cloud and air depend on our technological inventions.

All these natural elements that go in our food production are available for free. Earth, water, air and light are freely available in all parts of the world. Where is the question of farming becoming a colossal industry, requiring billions of dollars in investment.

If this is all true, then what is the role of agricultural universities and multi-trillion dollar agribusinesses? What is the role of government subsidies and international trade agreements. Why

people have to starve when they can grow their own food with simple efforts in any part of the world.

A Forest is a proof of nature's prefect and complete system. Since time immemorial, forest eco-systems have existed, producing fruits, flowers, herbs and honey. No agricultural scientist was ever required to maintain these delicate system. Neither there was any need for chemical or organic fertilizers, insecticides, cultivation by tractor, irrigation or GMO seeds. Nature, when left to itself, takes care of everything. Even trees in our countryside produce fruits year after year without any attention on our part.

Experts admit that natural soils are rich in nutrients but they emphasize chemical fertilizers because these nutrients in their natural form can not be utilized by the plant roots. The plant roots can not make use of them in spite of their abundant availability. The soil testing report may say that there is enough Potash in the soil but it is in an unavailable form. So we have to add it from outside.

That is where micro-organisms and friendly creatures like earthworms come into picture. They convert soil nutrients from their non-available form to available form. Just like we can not eat wheat unless it is converted into a bread.

In a forest system, soil is teeming with micro-organisms and therefore their is no necessity of any external input.

However, in our modern farms these nutrients (in acceptable format) are not available because the micro-organisms who convert these non-available nutrients are destroyed by poisonous chemical fertilizers, insecticides, fungicides, herbicides etc. It's like if you don't cook at home, you have to get your dinner from a restaurant. When soil's innate capacity to generate nutrients is impaired, we have to add artificial nutrients from outside.

If we want to avoid unhealthy restaurant food, we have to establish home cooking. Same way if we have to facilitate generation of nutrients within farm soil, then there will be no necessity of adding fertilizers externally.

How can we re-establish these micro-organisms in the soil? This is done by applying the cow dung of local cow. The cow dung of the local cow is a miraculous culture. As we add a spoonful of curd (culture) to a pot of milk , likewise the local cow dung is a culture for the whole field. One gram of cow dung contains about 3000 to 5000 million beneficial microbes.

How much cow dung is needed for one acre of land? Subash Palekar researched this subject for six years. He studied all Indian cow breeds like Gaulao, Lal Kandhari, Khilar, Deoni, Dangi, Nimari from Maharashtra; Gir, Tharparkar, Sahiwal, Redsindhi from West India; Amrutmahal, Krishna kathi from South India and Hariyana from North India. He tested the dung and urine of all these breeds on every crop, in each moon phase and constellation.

His first conclusion was that only dung from traditional local cows is effective, not from Holstein-Friesian breeds. We can mix half cow dung and half the dung of bullock or buffalo, but not of Jersey or Holstein at any cost.

Secondly, the cow dung and urine of black colored Kapila cow is most effective. Thirdly, the cow dung should be used as fresh as possible and the urine as old as possible. Fourthly, only one cow is needed for thirty acres of land. Farmer need not use any compost, vermi-compost for farmyard manure.

For one acre land, only ten kilogram of local cow dung is sufficient per month. One local cow gives on an average about 11 Kg of cow dung, one bullock about 13 Kg of dung and one buffalo about 15 Kg dung per day. For one acre one day's cow dung is enough. That means thirty days cow dung for thirty acres.

You can not imagine a forest without its fauna. To continually regenerate itself, a forest needs the excreta of the animals, birds, earthworms and insects. These inputs are necessary in any self-developing, self-nourishing system. That means the use of cow dung and urine is very natural and hence scientific.

Similar principal applies to this system of farming. Micro-organisms present in cow dung decompose the dried biomass in the soil and make the nutrients available to the plants. There is complete symbiosis in the nature. Jaggery is added in the mix to facilitate biological reaction.

The cow that gives more milk, its dung and urine are less effective and the cow that gives less milk, its dung and urine are more effective. *(Subash Palekar)*

Zero Budget Farming Preparations

Seed Treatment with Beejamrita
Composition:
a) Water 20 litres
b) Desi cow dung 5 kg
c) Desi cow urine 5 Litres
d) One handful of soil from the surface of field
e) Lime 50 grams

The above mixture termed as 'Beejamrita' can be used to treat seeds, seedlings or any planting material. The planting material has to be simply dipped in 'Beejamrita, taken out and planted. Beejamrita protects the crop from harmful soil borne and seed borne pathogens during the initial stages of germination and establishment.

Jeevamritam
Composition:
1) Water 200 litres
2) Desi cow dung 10 kg
3) Desi cow urine 5 to 10 litres
4) Jaggery 2 kg
5) Flour of any pulse 2 kg
6) Handful of soil from farm or forest -

The above mixture will suffice for one time application on one acre crop. 'Jeevamritam' is to be provided once in a fortnight or at least once in a month. It promotes immense biological activity in the soil and makes the nutrients available to the crop. Jeevamritam is not to be considered as nutrient for the crop but only a catalytic agent to promote biological activity in the soil.

Mulching

Mulching with organic residues or live mulching reduces tillage and consequently labour requirements, suppresses weeds, promotes humus formation and enhances the water holding capacity of the soil. Mulching enhances the biological activity and replenishes the nutrient base of the soil. Adequate mulching keeps the top and sub soil moist and enhances the water holding capacity of the soil and also reduces water loss due to evaporation so that the crop will be better equipped to tide over drought conditions.

Plant Protection

In the event of outbreak of insects and diseases the farmer can himself prepare home made pesticides and use it on the crops.

Fungicide-I

a) Butter milk fermented for five days 5 litres

b) Water 50 litres

Fungicide –II

a) Desi cow milk 5 litres

b) Black Pepper Powder 200 grams

c) Water 200 litres Insecticide- I

a) Powder of neem seed or Neem leaves 20 kg
b) Water 200 litres
Insecticide- II
a) Cow dung 5 kg
b) Cow urine 10 litres
c) Neem leaves 10 kg
d) Water 200 litres
This mixture is particularly effective against aphids, jassids, mealy bugs and white flies.
Insecticide – III
a) Neem leaves 10 kg
b) Tobacco powder 3 kg
c) Garlic paste 3 kg
d) Green chillies paste 4 kg

The above ingredients should be soaked in cow urine for ten days. About 3 litres of this mixture can be mixed with 100 litres of water and sprayed on crops.

The above mentioned fungicides and insecticides can be prepared by the farmer himself and used either as prophylactic or as curative measure for control of crop pests. If the economic injury to crops due to pests is less than five percent, it should be deemed to be 'return to nature' and no plant protection measures should be taken.

Mixed Cropping and Crop Rotation

Zero Budget Natural Farming advocates cultivation of diverse species of crops depending on site specific agro climatic conditions. Mixed cropping provides buffer against total failure of single crop and also widens the income source of farmers. There is stress on inclusion of leguminous crops to ensure replenishment of soil fertility. Crop rotation is also emphasized to discourage build up of endemic pests. In the scheme of mixed cropping, cereals, millets, leguminous crops, horticulture crops particularly vegetables and even medicinal plants can be included to make farming more lucrative.

The system also advocates wider spacing of crops to facilitate inter cropping. Palekar has repeatedly stressed that just as diversity is the rule of nature, the farm should also have diverse species.

Observations And Inferences

By R.Yogananda Babu

Visit to fields where Palekar's Zero Budget Natural Farming has been adopted and interaction with farmers whose profiles have been collected, revealed that all of them were raising crops using modern technology of improved seeds, fertilizers and plant protection chemicals before adopting this new method. They found the old method to be very cost intensive and by their own estimates the cost of cultivation of one acre of paddy was Rs.5000/- to Rs. 6000/- and that of sugarcane Rs. 15000/- to Rs. 20000/-.

Similarly the cost of cultivation of one acre of banana was Rs. 25,000/- to 30,000/-. This often compelled them to raise loan from conventional and institutional sources. However, the returns were not commensurate with the investments made for raising crops. The produce from field crops generally met the requirements of the family and the marketable surplus was not sufficient to repay the loan. Market forces were also some times detrimental to the interests of the farmers resulting in low price realization. It was evident from interaction with the selected farmers that they practiced a form of subsistence farming.

In this bleak scenario all the farmers selected for study attended orientation courses conducted by Subhash Palekar at different places of Karnataka. They were convinced that zero budget natural farming is farmer friendly, eco-friendly and above all extremely cost effective.

These reasons were cogent enough for them to give this method a fair trial and hence they switched over to this new method. The experience of the practicing farmers and field observations over a period of time lends credence to the following conclusions.

a) The system of zero budget natural farming is eminently suited to the farmers, particularly small and marginal farmers because of its simplicity, adoptability and drastic cut in cost of cultivation of crops. The appeal to the farming community lies in the fact that maintaining optimum levels of production and keeping the cost of cultivation to the bare minimum will substantially enlarge the profit margin.

All the sample farmers acknowledged it as farmer friendly and financially viable. However during the initial period of transition to new system, the results may not be encouraging because of the lingering effects of chemical farming. The results will become evident only after adequate mulching and restoration of biological activity in the soil. Hence, patience and perseverance are required on the part of farmers.

b) Treatment with Beejamrita and Jeevamrita has given extremely encouraging results for successful cultivation of crops. Beejamrita does provide adequate protection to crops from insects and diseases during the initial stages of germination and establishment. Mortality in case of treated crop is reported to be almost negligible.

The experience of the farmers bears ample testimony to the fact that Jeevamrita promotes rapid and enormous biological activity in the soil. However, it should be coupled with adequate mulching so that the soil is transformed into humus rich reservoir of nutrients. It is also observed that providing Jeevamrita once in a fortnight is better than providing it once in a month. It has been the experience of farmers that dispensing with the use of fertilizers has not adversely

"Modern agriculture is the use of land to convert petroleum into food. Without Petroleum we will not be able to feed the global population."
-Professor Albert Bartlett

affected crop yields. The use of home made pesticides has also been found to be effective in managing the crop pests without economic injury to crops.

c) Experience with this method of farming corroborates the fact that adequate mulching promotes humus formation, suppresses weeds and greatly reduces the water requirement of the crops. Live mulching particularly with leguminous crops has been found to be not only a subsidiary source of income but also a safeguard against depletion of nutrients by crops.

d) Mixed cropping particularly with short duration legumes, vegetables and even medicinal plants has certainly expanded the income source of farmers.

Vegetables rich in vitamins and minerals are generally marketed after adequately providing for home consumption and this certainly augurs well for overcoming malnutrition which is widespread in rural areas. Mr. Bannur Krishnappa obtained an additional income of more than Rs. 15,000/- by planting Ashwagandha and Coleus in one acre as intercrop with sugarcane.

e) All the farmers selected for study have expressed satisfaction that switching over to the new method from chemical agriculture has paid them good dividends.

Savings on cost of seeds, fertilizers and plant protection chemicals has been substantial. Almost all the farmers have stopped borrowing crop loan. They are also not depending on hired labour as the family labour is sufficient to carry out all the farming operations. The yields have been optimal with possibly no decline in future, because of continuous incorporation of organic residues and replenishment of soil fertility. The new system of farming has freed the farmers from the debt trap and it has instilled in them a renewed sense of confidence to make farming an economically viable venture. This is a noteworthy feature in an era marked with farmers committing suicide across the country.

Following reports on the success of zero budget farming were published in India's national newspapers.

Zero Budget Farming A Success

The Hindu, April 30, 2010

For A.C. Joshykumar of Muttukad in Bison Valley grama panchayat employing zero budget natural farming methods in his seven-acre multi-crops land has proved successful with considerable increase in yield.

Joshykumar is one of around 45 farmers in the district who have already shifted to zero budget farming, devised by Subhash Palekar of Amaravathy in Maharashtra.

Mr. Joshykumar said he could easily shift to zero budget farming since he had always practised organic farming methods. He said that full dedication and keen efforts were needed to shift to zero budget farming .

Zero budget farming proposes that only a single cow is needed to cultivate 30 acres of land. It employs scientific methods to rejuvenate the micro organisms in the soil with the help of earthworms.

India's civilization was based on village residence. They would live very peacefully in the villages. In the evening there would be bhagavata-katha. They will hear. That was Indian culture. They had no artificial way of living, drinking tea, and meat-eating and wine and illicit sex. No. Everyone was religious and satisfied by hearing -- what we are just introducing -- Bhagavatam, Bhagavad-gita, Puranas, and live simple life, keeping cows, village life as it is exhibited by Krsna in Vrndavana.

-Srila Prabhupada (Morning Walk -- Durban, October 13, 1975)

Fertilizers or pesticides are not used in the method. The focus of the cultivation is through the activation of micro organisms in the soil.

Mr. Joshyjkumar said that his main cultivation, pepper, is completely resisting pest attack even though he was not using any pesticides and production has increased considerably. He bought an indigenous variety of cow- Jaboo - from Kasargod when he shifted to this farming method.

Cow dung is the main component used for revitalising soil with the help of dried plants, which is used to cover the ground around the cultivated plants.

Besides pepper, he also cultivates vegetables, nutmeg and clove. "An exporting agent from Marayur who markets organic produce bought clove from me at Rs.400 a kg when the market price was Rs.310," he said.

Another farmer, Sunny Kudankavil of Panamkutty said he got an yield of 400 kg from 5 kg of ginger rizhome since he shifted to zero budget farming. "If you follow the guidelines suggested by Mr. Palekar, you will get the result," Mr. Kudankavil, who had attended a three-day workshop organised by Mr. Palekar said.

Though the Kerala Agriculture Development Society procures organic produce at 10 to 30 percent higher price, lack of a regular procurement scheme for organic produce is one problem faced by farmers, he said.

Jose Ammencheri, a cardamom farmer in Vandanmedu, said yield had not fallen when he shifted his 14-acre plantation to the new farming method. "There will not be a sudden increase in yield, but it sustains. Also, organic pest control methods are used," he said. Cardamom plantation is known for its high usage of pesticides.

V.C. Devasia said his cocoa plants and rubber plantation have shown higher yield since he shifted to zero budget farming three years ago.

Shaji Thundathil, who is co-ordinating the farmers engaged in zero budget farming, said that thousands of farmers were keen to shift to the farming method. He said that 300 acres of fallow grass land in Muttukadu would be cultivated using zero budget farming methods jointly by farmers, who have found success employing the method.

Zero-Budget Farming In Vithura, Kerala

The Hindu, Thiruvananthapuram, May 31, 2013

Farming is no 'hobby' for Abu Dhabi-based businessman Rohini Vijayan Nair from Vithura. Realising that the rooftop garden at his flat in Abu Dhabi is just too small for his experiments, this agri-enthusiast has now taken up farming in 100 acres of land at his hometown here.

"I needed to do a little more than terrace cultivation and thus took to farming in 100 acres of rubber plantation last year," says Mr. Nair, who manages to juggle farming in Kerala and business abroad.

Thanks to his effort and willingness to take up farming amidst his busy schedule, the land is now full of medicinal and indigenous plants, tropical trees, and various fruit trees along with rubber trees. He has also taken up banana and cashew cultivation.

But unlike other farmers, this man wanted to make sure that his farming techniques did not, in anyway, affect the natural pattern of the soil and land. The search for a suitable farming method finally ended with the zero-budget natural farming advocated by noted agricultural scientist Subhash Palekar.

"The method involves using locally obtainable natural bio-degradable materials and traditional techniques to improve fertility. Though it is not 'zero-budget' here as many other factors such as the State's climate and the labour cost have to be taken into account, it is a highly successful model," Mr. Nair says.

Test Farm

And for those who need proof of how beneficial and environment-friendly the method is, Mr. Nair has a test farm. In three sections of this land, he has been using bio-fertilisers, chemical fertilisers, and 'Jeevamritam' (fertilizer used for zero-budget farming), separately.

"When visitors ask me how nature-friendly the technique is, I want to show them the results of the three types of farming, their pros and cons. When they see the test farm and the produce, they themselves will understand how profitable budget farming is," Mr. Nair says. He has now joined hands with the Krishi Bhavan and has dedicated 25 acres of his land for vegetable cultivation, expecting to reap the harvest during Onam.

His date with farming does not end here. He takes classes for school children and organises field trips to his farm for them.

He says that many people have land but are not willing to cultivate. "But the younger generation is willing to listen and if we inculcate an interest in them, may be we can bring back what we have lost," Mr. Nair says.

47

Miracle of Cow Dung

The Fragrance Of Nature In Balance , New Zealand

Jon Morgan - Businessday, November 11, 2010

Ms Heather Smith, an American from the verdant eastern state of Vermont has made a home in New Zealand for the past 14 years. She lives at her picturesque farm in the shadow of Hawke's Bay's craggy Te Mata Peak.

She first heard about New Zealand as a university student in the 1980s.

She arrived in New Zealand in 1997, after working with groups in Vietnam, Taiwan, Hawaii and Alaska fighting to save endangered species, such as tigers and bears, and on habitat restoration projects.

Now, on her 275-hectare farm, she has a similar mission.

It is to help revive a way of life that she fears has been almost submerged by the drive for greater productivity at any cost.

She is concerned that farming is becoming too industrialised at the expense of the small family unit, of environmental and animal health and of urban shoppers' knowledge of where their food comes from and what goes into the making of it.

Her farm is an eclectic mix of sheep, cattle, chickens, feijoas, grain crops and truffle trees, all grown organically using the principles of early 20th-century philosopher Rudolf Steiner.

Known as biodynamics, the farming methods shun all synthetic chemicals, replacing them with compost and manure fertiliser nurtured in buried cow horns, and follow the phases of the moon and planets in planting crops.

"I know it sounds wacky," Ms Smith says, "but it works for me. *There's a feeling here of nature in balance. It's hard to explain, but there's a fragrance in the air - the trees, the soil, the animals, everything just smells right. People who come here tell me their souls feel so much better."*

She was travelling by train from Napier to Wellington when she first encountered biodynamics. Seated near her was a family with a bucket of worms. The worms were a gift from pioneering Kiwi biodynamics soil scientist Peter Proctor to the family. "I sat there with them for the whole five-hour trip, talking and learning. They were so smart, really into it."

Inspired by her encounter with the family, she began to learn more about biodynamics by reading and talking to practitioners.

With the help of farm manager Nick Radly, she gradually began to change the farm over to the new regime.

An essential part is the use of Steiner's Preparation 500, made by filling a cow horn with cow dung and burying it in autumn to be

dug up in spring. The cow horn is a keratin-rich container and it is filled with beneficial material from one of nature's most complex digestive systems. She describes the contents of the retrieved horn as fine, silky dirt. "It doesn't look like manure any more. It's full of beneficial fungi and bacteria."

A teaspoon of the preparation is stirred into 40 to 60 litres of warm water and sprayed on pasture to "kick the soil organisms into activity".

She calls on a science analogy to explain it. "It's like taking a swab from a strep throat and making a culture of the bugs in agar in a petri dish. On the farm, that's the cow horn of manure. In the dish, you can see the bacteria expand rapidly. And on the farm the same thing is happening when we've sprayed the bugs around. The difference is we're using good bugs."

The spray stimulates the soil biology, which leads to the growth of more nutrient-rich pastures, crops and garden vegetables and fruit, she says.

On her farm, this is seen in healthier animals and pastures. "The cows and sheep are more fertile, the sheep have less flystrike, I don't need to worm the horses, thistle numbers have plummeted

This Solution Could Make Paddy More Resistant To Pests
The following was taken from the daily, The Hindu, October 22, 2009.
"Dilute one litre of cow's urine in about 5 litres of water, take paddy seeds required for an acre and tie them into several small bundles and dip them in the solution for half an hour then dry the seeds under shade before sowing. Using this method several farmers have been successful and able to record that the seeds have become more resistant to infestations from pest attacks!"
With a mindful application the farmers, may be able to avoid the cost of pesticides, delivering a less harmful product to the consumer at a cheaper cost!

and the pastures hold on to water longer and stay greener longer in summer." It meant they coped better in the recent droughts, not being forced to sell stock. A low stocking rate and more than 7000 trees for shade and shelter also helped.

The soil is dark, crumbly and full of worms. Grass roots go deep and a clay pan is gradually being broken up. "People who come here, curious about what's happening, dig a hole, look at my soil and go, 'Ooh, aah'," she says.

Other fertilisers are lime, a worm-based compost tea and a variety of composts made from horse, cow and sheep manure, food scraps, basalt dust and Steiner preparations using camomile to stop nitrogen from leaching, yarrow to help the absorption of potassium and sulphur, nettles to promote iron and magnesium, dandelion for silica and valerian for phosphorus.

She has 300 ewes and 220 cattle of varying ages and takes 150 dairy grazers at a time.

At weaning, the cattle are given a black walnut remedy to reduce stress. "Every year, it gets easier," Ms Smith says and adds with a laugh, "and this year I swear the calves ran from their mothers."

The feijoas are a big future hope. She sells them to a juicer and an ice-cream maker, getting $1.30 a kilogram for her organically grown fruit, as against 70 cents for conventionally grown.

"It's a gem of a fruit," she says. "It's made into juice and pulp and all through the process retains its unique taste character, much more than other fruits."

However, the local market is saturated and export sales are needed to grow the industry.

She has seen the demand for organic food grow enormously and is frustrated that more is not being done to encourage organic farming. "It's crazy," she says. "The Government is allowing the science institutes to spend money on genetic engineering research when there's no demand for it. Why can't that money go into organics, which is in hot demand?"

She has a favourite saying: "We don't photosynthesize - we are what we eat. More and more people are coming to realise that. They don't want chemicals in their food. They want natural goodness."

Thirteen years on from her first experiments with biodynamics, she feels she is still learning.

"We're still in an establishment phase and I don't know how long that will last, but every year it is a little easier. There is a cost to it, though, and it can be difficult some years to keep your head above water."

An endless stream of wwoofers (Willing Workers on Organic Farms) flock her farm. "They're fabulous workers, so keen. They care so much for the planet and they come here to get back to nature, learn how to milk a cow, make cheese and bake bread - and hopefully spread the word as they travel. It's really inspiring."

48

Cow Dung Makes A Difference

Of Life And Death

A Tale Of Two Farmers

Here we narrate the story of two farmers who live in the same area in south India. One is happy and prosperous and the other is broke and dead. These reports were published in the newspapers on the same day.

Lankan Farmers Take Lessons In Cow Based Farming

Decca Herald, February 11 2012

A delegation of farmers from Sri Lanka visited farm of natural farmer Ramesh Raju at Kurahatti, Karnataka India last week.

Raju has succeeded in reaping good yield by adopting natural farming. Instead of fertiliser and other stimulants, Raju uses cow urine, cow dung cakes and jaggery to increase productivity of crops like banana and sugarcane.

Sharing his success story with his Sri Lankan counterparts - led by Jayant Tilak on a study tour, Raju said he cultivated 50 tonnes of sugarcane on one acre of land, spending Rs. 30,000. He has already earned Rs. 50,000 by growing sub-crops like brinjal, chilly and others.

In India with small holdings and small scale farming, there is no better alternative to employing cattle in farming.

While ploughing, the oxen stride with gentle gait, not harming the surface of the earth, unlike tractors.

Even as they plough the land, the oxen defecate and urinate, fertilising the land.

Cattle Manure : organic manure, green leaf manure, earth-worms, and slurry manure with cattle manure bond with the nature and make the land fertile. They do not create the challenge of chemical waste.

99% of the pests in nature are beneficial to the system. Insecticides prepared from cow urine or well fermented butter milk do not affect these helpful pests.

Dung from one cow is adequate to fertilise upto 30 acres of land and its urine can protect upto 10 acres of crops from insects.

The sugarcane expected to be harvested in five months will help produce 50 quintals of jaggery. According to the prevailing price jaggery costs Rs 3,500 per quintal.

He advised the delegates to adopt natural farming as propagated by Subhash Palekar (based on cow dung and urine) - invest less and earn more without depending on fertilisers or pesticides. "Already five workshops have been conducted in Sri Lanka. It was the workshop that aroused the curiosity of farmers and hence we are on a study tour. We will also urge the government to adopt natural farming to increase food production to meet the growing demand," he said.

The delegation included Sri Lanka Farmers' Association president Darshan de Silva and Subramanya Pillai among others.

Two Farmers Commit Suicide In State

Deccan Herald, February 11 2012

Two farmers, unable to repay debts, commit suicide in separate incidents on Saturday.

Venkate Gowda, 65, a resident of Hosakote village in Pandavapura taluk of Mandya district, committed suicide by consuming insecticide at his field in the morning. The villagers, who saw him writhing in pain, rushed him to the district hospital.

Joys of Cow Based Farming

Indian agriculture has variety. There is no farm-product that Indians don't cultivate. This land grows all kinds of grains, pulses, vegetables, fruits, flowers, cotton and silk.

About 70% of Indian population depend on agriculture for their livelihood. Majority of them are small farmers, owning one or two acres of land.

Indian agricultural landscape is diverse and vivid – in land topology, soil type and quality, irrigation method and frequency of harvesting.

Cattle are integral part of this huge canvas of agriculture. We use oxen to plough, to pick and move harvested crops and in irrigation. Cow manure is used as fertiliser, and cow urine as insecticide.

Both Ramesh Raju and Venkate Gowda's villages are about 6 kilometers distance.

Now what is the differences between these two farmers?

The difference is in their methods of farming. And these methods make a difference of life and death.

We require something, some because we have got this body. Very easy solution is given by Lord Krsna: annad bhavanti bhutani [Bg. 3.14]. You produce foodgrains. Why you are going to produce tools and implements and... Of course, we do not condemn. But at the sacrifice of producing foodgrains, we simply open big, big tire factory. When I go to Delhi I see, from Vrndavana, hundreds and thousands persons are coming from the village on cycle to go to the tire factory, Goodyear tire factory. So now eat tire instead of getting food grains. So this is misdirected civilization. Krsna does not say that you produce tire tube. Krsna says annad bhavanti bhutani: "You produce anna." This is practical solution. We have therefore started in Europe and America farming. And they are very happy. In our latest Back to Godhead the description is published about our farm in France. We have got a very palatial building. We have named it New Mayapur. What is the place?

Hari-sauri: Chateau d'Oublaise.

Prabhupada: I cannot pronounce this French word. So anyway, our men, there are about three hundred men living there. Last time, four months, five months before I was there. It is a very very nice place. We are getting our own fruits, own vegetables fresh, and we are getting fresh wheat and milk. It is so happy life.

So government is also advertising "Go to the village." Actually that is life. Go to the village. Mahatma Gandhi also wanted to organize this life, but unfortunately you have changed. Now we have got place in Hyderabad about six hundred acres of land. We are also trying here. We have already done in Mayapur. We are producing our own food, our own cloth, own milk, and we are chanting Hare Krsna. This is the simplest life. This life is meant for not working like hogs and dogs.

~ Srila Prabhupada (Srimad-Bhagavatam 5.5.1 -- Bombay, December 25, 1976)

49

Magic of Cow Dung

Story of A Lone Crusader

In November 2012, Indian government told the Supreme Court in an affidavit that it could not achieve the goal of reducing the number of hungry people by half without taking recourse to genetically modified (GM) crops, which could herald the second green revolution in the country. The central government said GM crops would not only lead to increased food security but would also reduce pressure on land use.

The central government pronounced its position backing field trials of GM crops while junking the interim report of the court-appointed Technical Expert Committee (TEC) report, which had recommended a 10-year moratorium on GM crops field trials.

But what about the farmers who are growing much more per acre than Mosanto or its forefathers can ever imagine? They are being conveniently ignored by the mainstream agricultural establishment. Why not make their techniques available to the masses?

G. Nagarathanam Naidu is one such farmer, based in South India, in Hyathnagar mandal near Hyderabad. He is producing 15.5 tons of rice per hectare by using indigenous cow based inputs in his field. His consumption of seeds, water, labour and other inputs is also much lower compared to other farmers. His methodology is given below.

Cropping System

- A combination of Zero Budget Natural Farming (ZBNF) and System of Rice Intensification (SRI)
- Application of farmyard manure (cow, sheep and goat manure) @ 5 tons/acre.
- Incorporation of Green manure and green leaf manure (Neem).
- Application of jeevamritham directly or along with farmyard manure to soil twice as top dressing.
- Using 2 kg seed for transplanting one acre, instead of 30 kg normally used.
- Planting 12 day old seedlings.
- Planting at 25x25cm spacing.
- Running three Row Cono weeder four times.
- Adopting alternate wetting and drying
- Controlling pests and diseases with bio-dynamic formulations, neem kernel
- Formation of irrigation channels round the field and for every 2 meters which are interconnected to save on irrigation water.

Jeevamritham Composition:

10kg cow dung
10 lit of cow Urine
0.5kg cow ghee
1kg jaggery
200g virgin red soil
Mixed in 200 lit of water
Application of bio-fertilizers (Azospirillum, Azotobacter, Phosphorus Solubilising bacteria) along with farmyard manure as top dressing.

Benefits

- Radical improvement in the soil health.
- Saving larger quantities of seeds i.e., 28kg seeds per acre
- Saving of irrigation water by 40% compared to conventional practice
- Higher yields for national food security.
- Overall cost of cultivation reduced by 25 percent.
- Increases yields by 30 percent over conventional practices.

G. Nagarathanam Naidu hails from a remote village Balakrishnapuram in Chittoor district, Andhra Pradesh. After obtaining his diploma in electronics, he took up a job but that could not satisfy his innate desire to be connected with the land. It was then he and his wife decided to acquire 17 acres of barren and rocky land on the outskirts of Hyderabad. They could not afford better land.

The couple converted their new land into a gold mine by sheer hard work. They now have a mini forest with its own micro-climate. They also practice floriculture and grow varieties of exotic fruits and other crops.

He travels to different parts of India to train other farmers. Students from various schools and colleges also visit his farm to learn something about natural farming.

Awards And Appreciations

Various dignitaries have visited his farm which include scientists from various countries and Chief Minister of Andhra Pradesh.

When the former US President George Bush visited India, he was allowed to interact with him as a farmers' representative.

In 2005, he received appreciation from the WWF international Project. In 2007, he was given a certificate of appreciation by Association for Land reforms and Development, Dhaka, Bangladesh. In 2008, he was give a letter of honor by ICRISAT for implementing organic farming practices in groundnut cultivation and generating a record yield.

Also he received a Letter of Appreciation from Jara Agro Industrial PLC, Ethiopia, in the year 2011 for his sincere efforts in educating the local farming community on high yield strategies and innovative techniques.

Recently he was honored as the "Best SRI Farmer" by WWF Netherlands in collaboration with ICRISAT.

50

Cow Dung And Farming

In A Low-Energy Future

We are eating oil and drinking oil. Oil is at the heart of industrial food production and processing, and long distance food transport. The systems that produce the world's food supply are heavily dependent on fossil fuels. Vast amounts of oil and gas are used as raw materials and energy in the manufacture of fertilisers and pesticides, and as cheap and readily available energy at all stages of food production: from planting, irrigation, feeding and harvesting, through to processing, distribution and packaging. In addition, fossil fuels are essential in the construction and the repair of equipment and infrastructure needed to facilitate this industry, including farm machinery, processing facilities, storage, ships, trucks and roads. The industrial food supply system is one of the biggest consumers of fossil fuels and one of the greatest producers of greenhouse gases.

Food security is increasingly coming under scanner in recent years as the law of diminishing returns sets in agriculture. How long our fields can support chemical inundation and reckless cultivation methods like monocroping.

Year 2007 saw "great wheat panic" grip the world and year 2008 is witnessing rationing of rice in USA, of all places, and food riots in dozens of countries.

More than oil, its "cheap" oil that is crucial for the survival of modern food industry. Virtually all of the processes in the modern food system are dependent upon this finite resource, which is nearing its depletion phase.

Not only is the contemporary food system inherently unsustainable, increasingly, it is damaging the environment.

Proximity and localisation of food system would be beneficial. Ironically, the food industry is at serious risk from global warming caused by these greenhouse gases, through the disruption of the predictable climactic cycles on which agriculture depends.

Environmental degradation, water shortages, salination, soil erosion, pests, disease and desertification all pose serious threats to our food supply, and are made worse by climate change.

Industrial agriculture and the systems of food supply are also responsible for the erosion of communities throughout the world. This social degradation is compounded by trade rules and policies, by the profit driven mindset of the industry, and by the lack of knowledge of the faults of the current systems and the possibilities of alternatives. But the globalisation and corporate control that

seriously threaten society and the stability of our environment are only possible because cheap energy is used to replace labour and allows the distance between producer and consumer to be extended.

However, this is set to change. Oil output is expected to peak in the next few years and steadily decline thereafter. We have a very poor understanding of how the extreme fluctuations in the availability and cost of both oil and natural gas will affect the global food supply systems, and how they will be able to adapt to the decreasing availability of energy. In the near future, environmental threats will combine with energy scarcity to cause significant food shortages and sharp increases in prices - at the very least. We are about to enter an era where we will have to once again feed the world with limited use of fossil fuels. But do we have enough time, knowledge, money, energy and political power and will to make this massive transformation to our food systems when they are already threatened by significant environmental stresses and increasing corporate control?

Just how energy inefficient the food system is can be seen in the crazy case of the Swedish tomato ketchup. Researchers at the Swedish Institute for Food and Biotechnology analysed the production of tomato ketchup. The study considered the production of inputs to agriculture, tomato cultivation and conversion to tomato paste (in Italy), the processing and packaging of the paste and other ingredients into tomato ketchup in Sweden and the retail and storage of the final product. All this involved more than 52 transport and process stages.

The aseptic bags used to package the tomato paste were produced in the Netherlands and transported to Italy to be filled, placed in steel barrels, and then moved to Sweden. The five layered, red bottles were either produced in the UK or Sweden with materials form Japan, Italy, Belgium, the USA and Denmark. The polypropylene

(PP) screw-cap of the bottle and plug, made from low density polyethylene (LDPE), was produced in Denmark and transported to Sweden. Additionally, LDPE shrink-film and corrugated cardboard were used to distribute the final product. Labels, glue and ink were not included in the analysis.

Another example of how much fossil fuel goes into our food is our sandwich:

1. And we look first at the bread: we have to plant the cereal using a diesel tractor – this means ploughing, harrowing, drill the seeds. Then in conventional farming we add a load of chemicals to make it grow, and to protect the crop we add fungicides, herbicides, insecticides, all made from oil. Then extra nutrients in the form of chemical food is given, derived from natural gas. Then the wheat is harvested, and then driven to be processed.

2. If it is not a vegetarian sandwich, then the meat it contains has more fossil fuel in it. Cows and pigs are even more energy hungry in that they are fed on grains.

3. Now the salad – this is either shipped or flown or grown in a heated greenhouse which uses a huge amount of energy.

4. Then is this is all either cooked or cooled or both and driven miles and miles before being assembled into a sandwich.

Basically the sandwich is dripping in oil as a result of the way our food production is today. We will starve if we have no oil refineries.

Farming and food production without oil will grind to a halt.

This example demonstrates the extent to which the food system is now dependent on national and international freight transport.

However, there are many other steps involved in the production of this everyday product. These include the transportation associated with: the production and supply of nitrogen, phosphorous and potassium fertilisers; pesticides; processing equipment; and farm machinery. It is likely that other ingredients such as sugar, vinegar, spices and salt were also imported. Most of the processes listed above will also depend on derivatives of fossil fuels. This product is also likely to be purchased in a shopping trip by car.

Food production is going to be an enormous problem in the Long Emergency. As industrial agriculture fails due to a scarcity of oil- and gas-based inputs, we will certainly have to grow more of our food closer to where we live, and do it on a smaller scale.

The priority must be the development of local and regional food systems, preferably organically based, in which a large percentage of demand is met within the locality or region. This approach, combined with fair trade, will ensure secure food supplies, minimise fossil fuel consumption and reduce the vulnerability associated with a dependency on food exports (as well as imports). Localising the food system will require significant diversification, research, investment and support that have, so far, not been forthcoming. But it is achievable and we have little choice.

Farming In A Low-energy Future.

An approaching energy crisis will affect what we eat, where it comes from and even the alarming question of whether there will be enough food to keep us fed. If we are to survive we will have to change.

And it seems that the sooner we begin that transition to a new low energy future the easier the task will be.

51

Rwandan Agriculture

Growing One Cow At A Time

Rwanda, a conflict torn fragile state of yesteryears is boasting of peace and security, demonstrating food security and leading regionally in aid management and on governance issues. The reforms and efforts in the agriculture sector are a major part of this transformation. And behind this transformation of a nation stands the humble cow, munching grass and looking curious.

One of the most compelling stories has been that of the process of agricultural transformation. Agriculture is an unmovable cornerstone of Rwandan society. Eighty percent of the people depend on the land for their livelihoods. The land scarcity and the fact that Rwanda has one of the highest population densities in Africa, culminate in farming being conducted by smallholders who own, on average, 0.5 hectares of farmland.

'With a high population density and a lack of cultivatable unoccupied land, farmer productivity increases are paramount. With this in mind, the Ministry of Agriculture and Animal Resources

designed the Crop Intensification Program.

One Cow Per Family - The Girinka Program

Parallel to the Crop Intensification program and equally as important in dealing with poverty, and definitely more powerful in dealing with malnutrition, is the One Cow per Poor Family Program—locally known as the Girinka Program.

'This program like many other initiatives in Rwanda has deep roots in the Rwanda culture: where malnutrition in kids is a shame to family and society and where sharing a cow (passing on an offspring to other families) builds very strong society bonds.

The Girinka Program, started by the President in 2006, has secured a productive asset in the hands of poor farmers and mitigated child malnutrition with milk drinking. The program now targets about 350,000 poor families across the country of whom 92,000 have already received a cow. This program has locally been scored as most successful of all economic uplifting programs at the household level. The externalities are enormous; besides dealing with malnutrition, farmers have income from the sale of extra milk and offsprings from the cow, they access manure for their land—a factor that has seen crop and livestock very neatly integrated in Rwanda.

The most powerful externality however, is at the society level; a farmer who receives a cow passes on the first female offspring to another needy farmer. This has built a strong sense of community bonding that Rwanda needs very badly. Recently, the IFAD [International Fund for Agricultural Development] President was visiting farmers in Rwanda and one beneficiary of a cow from an IFAD supported project proudly showed him his bank book. The President asked him there was anything that IFAD could do to improve his life even more and the farmer said "Yes, give a cow to my neighbours who are still waiting their turn."

One Cow Per Family Programme is set to expand to reach those most in need over the next three years.

"Human society needs only sufficient grain and sufficient cows to solve its economic problems. All other things but these two are artificial necessities created by man to kill his valuable life at the human level and waste his time in things which are not needed."
~Srila Prabhupada (Srimad Bhagavatam 3.2.29)

52

Cuba And Cows

The Lessons Learnt

Cows have a rich history in Cuba. Spanish conquistador Diego Velazquez, the former governor of Cuba, brought 970 cows to the island in the years 1512 to 1524. Their numbers multiplied. By the mid-1500s, cattle hide had replaced gold as the main currency of exchange in Cuba.

From then on, the cattle industry was the No. 1 source of income to the Cuban economy up to the end of the 18th century, From

about 1800 until 1958, there was at least one cow for every person in Cuba.

After the revolution, the government confiscated all cattle farms larger than 66 acres. Sugar production became the priority and the number of cows dwindled.

The agriculture also took a plunge during the period and Cuba became a net food importer to feed its 11 million people.

Arturo Riera, president of the National Association of Cuban Cattlemen says, "Before the revolution, you could see cows all over, everything has changed. The number of cows has plunged from 6.3 million in 1958 to less than 2 million today. The regime did nothing to prevent the slaughter of countless head of cattle. Now they buy 50 cows from USA. That's not going to do a darn thing. You cannot improve an industry that had more than 6 million cows overnight. It will take years to restore the Cuban cattle industry to its former grandeur."

Golden Cows of Cuba - "I'm worth more than you"

But there has been an awakening in Cuba. Today the cows are sacred in Cuba. A colorful etching spotted at an Old Havana crafts market underscored that point, depicting a cow saying, "I'm worth more than you."

That's because a person can get more jail time for killing a cow than killing a human, under Cuban law. Cow killers can get four to 10 years in prison under a toughened crime law. Those who transport or sell the meat from an illegally slaughtered cow can get three to eight years. Providing beef at an unauthorized restaurant or workplace can fetch two to five years. And buying contraband beef is punishable by three months to one year in jail or a steep fine. Authorities also have the power to confiscate all or part of the property of anyone involved in black-market cattle dealings.

In contrast, the jail sentence for homicide is generally seven to 15 years, unless there are aggravating circumstances. Suspects involved in contract hits, kidnap-murders, sadistic or perverse killings, the murder of police officials and other acts can get from 15 years in jail to the death penalty.

A Cuban cow called Ubre Blanca holds the world record in milk production. In 1982, the cow produced 28 gallons of milk in a day, about four times more than average. Later, it produced 6,309 gallons in 305 days. Both are world records. The cow died in 1985. Meanwhile, the animal has been stuffed and is on display at Cuba's cattle institute.

Milk remains in short supply in Cuba and is rationed. Mothers with infants younger than 1 are allowed to buy containers of milk for about 2 cents, a heavily subsidized price. Families with pregnant women or children younger than 7 can buy 2.2-pound bags of powdered milk for less than 10 cents. All other Cubans pay the market price. A container of milk goes for $1.45.

Cuba is also taking lead in preparing for post-petroleum farming. In Cuba, the ox is mightier than the tractor. Ox is viewed as way to ramp up food production while conserving energy. Cuba may rely more heavily than ever on oxen to save fuel normally used by heavy machinery.

President Castro is promoting the draft animals as a way for the economically strapped communist country to ramp up food production while conserving energy. He recently suggested expanding a pilot program that gives private farmers fallow government land to cultivate - but without the use of gas-guzzling machinery.

"For this program we should forget about tractors and fuel, even if we had enough. The idea is to work basically with oxen," Castro told parliament on Aug. 1, 2009. "An increasing number of growers have been doing exactly this with excellent results."

Though the island gets nearly 100,000 free barrels of oil a day from Venezuela, it also has begun a campaign to conserve crude. The agricultural ministry in late June proposed increasing the use of oxen to save fuel. The ministry said it had more than 265,000 oxen "capable of matching, and in some cases overtaking, machines in labor load and planting."

In the farming initiative that began last year, about 82,000 applicants have received more than 1.7 million acres so far — or 40 percent of the government's formerly idle land. Shortages in Cuba are not new. And neither are oxen. Thousands of Cuban farmers have relied on the beasts in the half century since Fidel and Raul Castro took over the country. "The ox means so much to us. Without oxen, farming is not farming," says Omar Andalio, 37, as he carefully coaxes a pair of government-owned beasts through a sugarcane field.

53

India

Cow Killing And Death of A Great Civilization

India of yore is examplified by Vrindavan, an ancient pastoral village. Vrindavan is a typical representation of Vedic India, an India that was known all over the world for her immense wealth and a highly advanced culture. Cows formed the backbone of it and cows were such an inseparable part of its daily life that Indian culture can safely be termed as cow culture.

When the British colonized India, they studied India thoroughly to keep her under subjugation. The Governor of British India, Robert Clive extensively studied Indian economic and agricultural systems. He found that India was firmly footed in its age-old customs and sound agricultural practices, based on cow protection. We can quote a letter of Lord MCLau here, a British colonial dated February 2, 1835.

"I have traveled across the length and breath of India and I have not seen one person who is a beggar, who is a thief, such wealth I have seen in this country, such high moral values, people of such caliber (of noble character), that I do not think we would ever conquer this country...........unless we break the very backbone of this nation which is her spiritual and cultural heritage."

During his surveys in 1740, Robert Clive found that in Arcot District of Tamil Nadu, 54 Quintals of rice was harvested from one acre of land using manure and pesticides from cow urine and cow dung. Cow was the foundation of this nation and cows greatly outnumbered men. He realized that unless this foundation was shaken up, they could not keep their hold on India for too long. This inspired him to open his first slaughterhouse in India in 1760, with a capacity to kill thousands of cows every week. As a part of the master plan to destabilize India, cow slaughter was initiated. To this extent, the British were quite successful. Cow slaughter, engineered by them, divided Hindu and Muslim communities which had coexisted peacefully for the last 700 years. Millions died in ensuing riots which lasted for decades. To this day, India and Pakistan are locked in bitter enmity and are continuously suffering.

Robert Clive started a number of slaughter houses before he left India. By 1910, 350 slaughterhouses were working day and night. India was reduced to severe poverty, millions were dying from hunger and malnutrition, age-old cottage industries were devastated and village artisans took up jobs as coolies in cities. Manchester cloth effectively destroyed Indian handlooms industry. Using Indian money and Indian man power, the British were expanding their empire all over the world.

Bereft of its cattle wealth, India had to approach England for industrial manure. Thus industrial manure like urea and phosphate made way to India. Indian villages, in which once flowed streams of milk and butter, became haunted hamlets, wretched and starving. A Paradise was lost. An India where horses and bullocks were made to drink ghee, was now suffering from the scarcity of margarine. It was total devastation of a great civilization.

The British established an educational system which decried anything connected with Indian tradition. This was a crafty engineering by Macaulay who said, "We must at present do our best to form a class of persons Indian in blood and colour but English in tastes, in opinion, in morals, and in intellect." He did this so effectively that even after sixty years of independence Indians still continue to exist in a state of stupor, unable (and even unwilling!) to extricate themselves from one of the greatest hypnoses woven over a whole nation.

By the time British departed from India, thousands of slaughterhouses were in operation and now after independence, its

hard to keep a count of them. Instead of there being improvement in the well-being of cow, as was expected after the departure of the British, the suffering of the cow only multiplied. A large responsibility for this falls on the post-1950 policies of the Government of India.

The result - 40000 suicides by Indian farmers every year, failing agriculture and highest number of malnourished children in the world.

Indian government is proud of the fact that India today is the largest beef exporter in the world. It is introducing factory farming in a big way and is completely oblivious of the fact that conditions in Western countries and India greatly differ and what may work there for sometime will not work here at all.

The uncivilized men, they cannot produce food; therefore they kill animal. In the forest they live, and they kill some animals and eat. They cannot... They have no such knowledge that the forest can be cleared and we can till the ground and we can get very nice foodstuff, foodgrains, vegetables, so many things. Krsi, agriculture. So the land is there, but these uncivilized men do not know how to get the necessities of life from land. They do not know. Otherwise, in the land everything is there. It is stated in the Srimad-Bhagavatam, Sarva-kama-dugha mahi. Kama, kama means the necessities. We can get all the necessities of our life from the land. The land is so important. But the uncivilized man, they do not know how to utilize the land. Therefore they commit sinful activities for their existence. Instead of utilizing land for the necessities of life, unnecessarily... Although they are civilized -- they should not have done so -- they are killing animals.

~ Srila Prabhupada (Lecture, Srimad-Bhagavatam 1.7.26 -- Vrndavana, September 2, 1976)

54

Sacred Mother Earth

And God-Centered Farming

The ecological crisis of the late 20th century displays a profound alienation from nature and indeed from matter itself. Because nature had become largely identified as matter which can be manipulated. Nature is seen as a "resource" to be used rather than a "source" of life to be respected. Our planet is struggling against unprecedented assaults that include environmental pollution, destruction of entire ecosystems, the aesthetic degradation of nature, human overpopulation, resource depletion, industrial growth, technological manipulation, military proliferation, and, now emerging as the most pressing and desperate of all problems, abrupt massive species extinction - and in cases of recently discovered ones, often before they are given names.[1]

We are "Killing our World" wrote botanist Peter H. Raven (1993). Our feeling of alienation in the modern period has extended beyond the human community and its patterns of material exchanges to our interaction with nature itself. Especially in technologically sophisticated urban societies, we have become removed from that recognition of our dependence on nature - we no longer see the earth as sacred.

Instead, we spend so much of our lives courting death. We are fomenting wars, watching with sickening horror, movies in which maniacs slice and dice their victims, or hurrying to our own deaths in fast cars, through cigarette smoking, or by committing suicide. Death obsesses us - our responses are so strange that we not only kill for food, we kill each other along with the natural forces that nourish life on this planet (P.O. Ingram, 1997)[1]

Agriculture And The Sacred

In ancient times agriculture was intimately connected with the sacred. We find evidence of this in a host of texts and in many traditions which survive to this day. We know, for example, that for the indigenous people on the American continent, the corn plant is believed to have come into being through a long process of cooperation between human beings and the gods, and to grow corn is still a sacred activity for many Native American people today.[2]

If we try to discern the ultimate source of these traditions, we discover that people in ancient cultures experienced the natural world much differently than we do. Where today we might see, for example, simply a corn plant (tall stem, tassels, ears, husks, silks, kernels, etc.), they saw the body of a spiritual being whom they felt to be the ultimate source of the unique traits and gifts of that particular plant species.[2]

Sacred Mother Earth

In the Atharvaveda, the earth is described in one hymn of 63 verses. This famous hymn called as Bhumisukta or Prithivisukta

"We have got experience. In sometimes we find in this mango season profuse mango. People cannot end it by eating. And sometimes there is no mango. Why? The supply is in the hand of Krsna through His agent, the material nature, this earth. The earth can produce profusely if people are honest, God conscious. There cannot be any scarcity. Therefore it is said that kamam vavarsa parjanyah [SB 1.10.4]. God gives. Eko yo bahunam vidadhati kaman. Nityo nityanam cetanas cetananam (Katha Upanisad 2.2.13). So God, Krsna, fulfills all our desires."

-Srila Prabhupada (Srimad-Bhagavatam 1.10.4, Mayapur, June 19, 1973)

indicates the environmental consciousness of the Vedic seers. She is called Vasudha for containing all wealth, Hiranyavaksha for having gold bosom and Jagato Niveshani for being abode of the whole world. She is not for the different races of mankind alone but for all living beings. She is called Visvambhara because she is representative of the universe. She is the only planet directly available to us for the study of the universe and to realize the underlying truth. The earth supports varieties of herbs, oceans, rivers, mountains, hills etc. She has different colours as dark, tawny, white. She is raised in some place and lowered in some places. The earth is fully responsible for our food and prosperity. She is praised for her strength. She is served day and night by rivers and protected by the sky. The immortal heart of earth is in the highest firmament (Vyoma).[3]

Her heart is the Sun. She is one enveloped by the sky or space and causing the force of gravitation. She is described as holding Agni, i.e. the geothermal field. She is also described as holding Indra i.e., the geomagnetic field. The earth is present in the middle of the oceans and having magical movements.

The hymns talk about different energies which are generated from the form of the earth. 'O Prithivi! Thy centre, thy navel, all forces that have issued from thy body- set us amid those forces; breathe upon us.' Thus, the earth holds almost all the secrets of nature, which help us in understanding the universe. She is invested with divinity and respected as mother. The earth is my mother and I am her son.[3]

Gaia Hypothesis

Gaia is the the primal Greek goddess personifying the earth. Gaia is a primordial deity in the ancient Greek pantheon and considered a mother Goddess.

Etymologically Gaia is a compound word of two elements. Ge, meaning "earth" and 'aia' is a derivative of an Indo-European stem meaning "Grandmother".

This epical name was revived in 1979 by James Lovelock, in 'Gaia: A New Look at Life on Earth' which proposed a Gaia hypothesis. The hypothesis proposes that living organisms and inorganic material are part of a dynamic system that shapes the earth's biosphere, and maintains the earth as a fit environment for life. In some Gaia theory approaches, the earth itself is viewed as an organism with self-regulatory functions. Further books by Lovelock and others popularized the Gaia Hypothesis, which was widely embraced and passed into common usage as part of the heightened awareness of environmental concerns of the 1990s.

Gaia has been widely held throughout history and has been the basis of a belief which still coexists with the great religions. Today the very word 'Gaia' has come to mean ecology and sustainability.

There is a thriving green community which runs the portal Gaia. com.

Interestingly, in India the cow is known as 'Gai' and Vedic literatures have similar words, 'Gau' or 'Gava'.

The word Gaia has been derived from these words. If we go to Nirukta, the earliest book of etymology from India, the two primary meanings of the word 'gau' from which 'gava' is derived, are given in the following order:

1. The planet earth
2. The animal, cow.

By using interchangeable words for cow and earth, Vedas, the oldest repository of knowledge, state that the cow is a symbolic representation of the earth. In almost all Indian languages, cow is knows as gai or go-mata.

Therefore cow has a serious significance for saving a planet in crisis. Of all the man-made crises, probably the worst is the destruction of top soil and desertification of fertile lands.

Isavasya (God-centered) Farming

By Rupanuga dasa

A God-centered farming conception is relevant because it forms the basis for a workable agricultural life-style which includes a strict consideration of the ecological balance between humans, animals, the land, and God. Although sophisticated modern farmers might concede that the success of their endeavors, including their use of innovative machinery, depends in the end on "acts of Providence or God," or at least upon chance, the Isavasya (God-centered) farmer considers that long-range production and ecological balance require actual God consciousness. Therefore, even today in many parts of India, farmers make a point of gratefully offering God a portion of the crop in the form of prasada, or vegetarian food preparations. These offerings are often part of community celebrations in which the members of the community or village meet, especially in the morning and evening, to chant God's holy names and dance.

This God-centered attitude does not reflect a "primitive" agrarian culture or mentality of a distant Indian sect, but about a life-style that's in real harmony with the ideals of sustainable living. In fact, some of the most successful of the modern farm communities are based expressly upon isavasya principles.

A holistic farm community doesn't use technological prowess to try to outwit natural laws. Rather, community members try to do their work in a God-conscious way. "Success cannot come by working at your own risk," says a community member, "You may get good results for a while, but lasting success depends on how conscious you are of your relationship with the actual proprietor of nature."

Gradually, we have to become aware that God is always present—in every place and at every moment. As we learn this art of being conscious of God's presence, we will naturally develop a devotional, serving attitude toward everyone, including humans, plants, and animals. Then we will see all living beings as spiritually equal, because all living beings are equally related with God. Thus, in one sense, returning to the land, to vegetarianism, to nonviolence, to herbal medicine, and to ecological concern— returning to nature—necessitates returning to God consciousness, our natural consciousness. The age-old Vedic literatures describe that consciousness, in clear-cut, scientific terms.

In fact, in most instances the work of scientists like Howard, Kervran, Baranger, and Hauschka echoes these Vedic conclusions. Howard, for example, simply rediscovered ancient, biologically sound, and ecologically balanced agrarian practices based upon Vedic principles. And Hauschka's assertion that life is not a combination of elements, that instead it "precedes" matter and "originates in a preexistent spiritual cosmos," tells us what the Vedic literatures said thousands of years ago. The Bhagavad-gita, the essence of the Vedas, verifies that individual life is never created or destroyed, but that it is moving (transmigrating) among temporary bodies sustained by God, the original life.[4]

Reference

1. The Rise and Fall of Western Dominance, Discussion Paper, Adam Lecture, Pierre Madl..

2.. Agriculture And The Sacared, Robert Karp, RSF Quarterly, Fall 2013

3. S.R.N. Murthy, Vedic View of the Earth, D.K, Printworld,Delhi, 1997

4. Rupanuga dasa, Isavasya (God-centered) Farming

5. James Lovelock, A New Look at Life on Earth', 1979

THE AUTHOR

Dr. Sahadeva dasa (Sanjay Shah) is a monk in Vaisnava tradition. His areas of work include research in Vedic and contemporary thought, Corporate and educational training, social work and counselling, travelling, writing books and of course, practicing spiritual life and spreading awareness about the same.

He is also an accomplished musician, composer, singer, instruments player and sound engineer. He has more than a dozen albums to his credit so far. (SoulMelodies.com)

His varied interests include alternative holistic living, Vedic studies, social criticism, environment, linguistics, history, art & crafts, nature studies, web technologies etc.

Many of his books have been acclaimed internationally and translated in other languages.

By The Same Author

Oil-Final Countdown To A Global Crisis And Its Solutions

End of Modern Civilization And Alternative Future

To Kill Cow Means To End Human Civilization

Cow And Humanity - Made For Each Other

Cows Are Cool - Love 'Em!

Let's Be Friends - A Curious, Calm Cow

Wondrous Glories of Vraja

We Feel Just Like You Do

Tsunami Of Diseases Headed Our Way - Know Your Food Before Time Runs Out

Cow Killing And Beef Export - The Master Plan To Turn India Into A Desert

Capitalism Communism And Cowism - A New Economics For The 21st Century

Noble Cow - Munching Grass, Looking Curious And Just Hanging Around

World - Through The Eyes Of Scriptures

To Save Time Is To Lengthen Life

Life Is Nothing But Time - Time Is Life, Life Is Time

Lost Time Is Never Found Again

Spare Us Some Carcasses - An Appeal From The Vultures

An Inch of Time Can Not Be Bought With A Mile of Gold

Career Women - The Violence of Modern Jobs And The Lost Art of Home Making

Cow Dung – A Down To Earth Solution To Global Warming And Climate Change

Corporatocracy - You Are A Corporate Citizen, A Slave of Invisible And Ruthless Masters

Working Moms And Rise of A Lost Generation

Glories of Thy Wondrous Name

India A World Leader in Cow Killing And Beef Export - An Italian Did It In 10 Years

As Long As There Are Slaughterhouses, There Will Be Wars

Peak Soil – Industrial Civilization, On The Verge of Eating Itself

If Violence Must Stop, Slaughterhouses Must Close Down

(More information on availability on DrDasa.com)

www.ingramcontent.com/pod-product-compliance
Lightning Source LLC
Chambersburg PA
CBHW060450280326
41933CB00014B/2719